Developing Your School's Student Support Teams

Developing Your School's Student Support Teams is a practical manual for schools seeking to establish and sustain coordinated teams in support of students' social, emotional and behavioral health. Every day, students struggle with a range of issues, including traumas, that complicate their learning, engagement and overall well-being. School psychologists, counselors, social workers and nurses are employed in many school districts, but their schedules often make it difficult to collaborate effectively in developing and implementing comprehensive intervention plans. This book promotes teamwork throughout schools by exploring how interdependent practitioners can come together at the appropriate levels and times to help coordinate school and community resources. This "filtering" process will guide K-12 leaders and service professionals toward systems and decision-making that enable long-term student supports, accurate identification of systemic learning barriers, improved school culture and climate, attention to diverse populations, and more. With these proactive teamwork strategies, school staff will be better prepared to share workload and accountability and to identify and build upon the existing strengths and supports of every student.

Steve Berta has taught the Organizational Change and Development courses in the Counselor Education Department at San Jose State University, USA. He previously served as Manager of Student Services in the San Jose Unified School District and was Director of Health Education and Safe and Drug Free Schools for the Santa Clara County Office of Education.

Howard Blonsky is a consultant in school mental health and student support services. He previously served as a school social worker and program consultant in the San Francisco Unified School District.

James Wogan is Assistant Director of Student Support Services in the Mt. Diablo Unified School District. He previously served as Director of Wellness in the Acalanes Union High School District and as Manager of Student Services in the Berkeley Unified School District.

Developing Your School's Student Support Teams

A Practical Guide for K-12 Leaders, Student Services Personnel, and Mental Health Staff

Steve Berta, Howard Blonsky, and James Wogan

Routledge
Taylor & Francis Group

NEW YORK AND LONDON

Cover image: Getty Images

First published 2022
by Routledge
605 Third Avenue, New York, NY 10158

and by Routledge
4 Park Square, Milton Park, Abingdon, Oxon, OX14 4RN

Routledge is an imprint of the Taylor & Francis Group, an informa business

Library of Congress Cataloging-in-Publication Data
Names: Berta, Steve, author. | Blonsky, Howard M., author. | Wogan, James, author.
Title: Developing your school's student support teams : a practical guide for K-12 leaders,
    student services personnel, and mental health staff / Steve Berta, Howard Blonsky, and James Wogan.
Description: New York, NY : Routledge, 2022. | Includes bibliographical references.
Identifiers: LCCN 2021040359 (print) | LCCN 2021040360 (ebook) | ISBN 9781032145334 (hardback) |
    ISBN 9781032146294 (paperback) | ISBN 9781003240266 (ebook)
Subjects: LCSH: Student assistance programs. | Students--Services for. | School psychology. |
    Educational counseling. | Affective education.
Classification: LCC LB3430.5 .B47 2022 (print) | LCC LB3430.5 (ebook) | DDC 371.7–dc23
LC record available at https://lccn.loc.gov/2021040359
LC ebook record available at https://lccn.loc.gov/2021040360

ISBN: 978-1-032-14533-4 (hbk)
ISBN: 978-1-032-14629-4 (pbk)
ISBN: 978-1-003-24026-6 (ebk)

DOI: 10.4324/9781003240266

Typeset in Optima
by SPi Technologies India Pvt Ltd (Straive)

Access the Support Material: www.routledge.com/9781032146294

Contents

Meet the Authors	ix
Preface	xi
Introduction and Overview	xiii

I School-Based Student Support Structures and the Multi-Level

Identification and Intervention Process 1

Multi-Tiered System of Support 1

Opportunities, Services and Supports 3

Student Support Team Structures and the Filtering/Funneling Process ... 4

Drawing Strength from Diversity 7

References 8

2 The School Coordinated Care Team (SCCT) 9

What is a Coordinated Care Team and Why do We Need One
at Our School? 9

When Can/Does Our Coordinated Care Team Meet? We are All
So Busy Already 11

Who will Be on Our Coordinated Care Team? 11

Who is in Charge of the Coordinated Care Team? 12

What are the Care Team's Roles and Responsibilities? 12

When a Student of Concern is Presented for Discussion Before the
Care Team, What is Expected to be Brought to the Meeting Table? ... 13

Does the Coordinated Care Team Structure Function the Same Way at the
Elementary, Middle or High School Levels? 14

What Would a Typical Care Team Agenda Look Like? 15

The Oath of Confidentiality 16

Contents

SCCT Tip Sheet 21
SCCT: Key Concepts 23
Resource Coordination Tips 24
References 25

3 The Student Success Team (SST) Philosophy and Implementation   26
Four Themes that are "Key" to the SST process 27
Getting Started 30
Looking at Behaviors through a New Lens 47
SST Frequently Asked Questions 47
References 50

4 School Attendance Review Team (SART)   51
Why Attendance Matters 51
Key Considerations for an Effective Attendance Program 53
Some Additional Considerations that Might be Impacting Attendance   54
A Multi-Tiered Approach to Attendance Improvement 54
Inviting Parent(s)/Guardian(s) to a SART Conference 57
The Tone of SART Conferences 58
Identifying and Addressing the Root Causes of Absenteeism ... 59
Effective Use of SART Contracts 60
Strategies for Improving Student Attendance 63
SART Frequently Asked Questions 65
References 67

5 Meeting Facilitation   69
The Role of the Facilitator and Facilitation 69
Key Concepts of Facilitation 70
Facilitation Skill Practice 71
Facilitation Assessment Checklist 71
Reference 72

6 The Benefits of Effective Teaming   73
The Characteristics of an Effective Team 74
Things People Like About Teams/Committees when they Function Well   74
Reasons Why People Do Not Like to Serve on Teams/Committees   75

7 Supporting and Serving Special Populations   76
Unhoused Students 76
Youth in Foster Care 77

Re-Engagement of Youth who are Disengaged or Have Dropped Out 78
Re-Entry Program Models 81
Reference 82

8 The Importance of School Climate and Culture 83
School Climate Inventory 84
School Climate and Culture in Relation to Students' Mental Health
and Well-Being 85
References 86

9 Case Management: A Creative Philosophy and Form of Practice 87
The Problem that Case Management Seeks to Address 87
Is the Term "Case Management" a User-friendly Term? 87
The Importance of the Relationship 88
Why Schools? 88
Case Management: A Definition for Schools 89
The Case Manager: A Definition 89
The Steps in the Case Management Process 90
Once Again, the "Broad Range of Interventions" 92
Core Principles of Case Management 94
Qualifications for Case Managers 94
Case (Care) Management: Key Concepts 95
Reference 96

10 Making the Home-School Connection a Positive One 97
Parent Communication and Involvement Tip Sheet 98
Examples of Unwelcoming School Experiences for Parents/Guardians 99
Parents/Guardians Feel Welcome to the School When 100
Some Possible Roles for Parents/Guardians in Schools 100

11 Positive Behavioral Support vs. the Punishment Paradigm 102
The Hurt that Troubled Children Create is Never Greater than the Hurt
that they Feel 104

List of Appendices 106
School Coordinated Care Team Flow Chart 107

Appendix 1: School Coordinated Care Team (SCCT) 110

Appendix 2: Student Success Team (SST) 117

Appendix 3: School Attendance Review Team (SART) 126

Meet the Authors

Steve Berta has taught the Organizational Change and Development, and Law and Ethics classes for the Counselor Education Department at San Jose State University. He previously served as the Manager of Student Services in the San Jose Unified School District and was Director of Health Education and Safe and Drug Free Schools for the Santa Clara County Office of Education. Steve also served as an elementary school teacher and principal on his career journey. (swbcruz@hotmail.com)

Howard Blonsky currently serves as a consultant in School Mental Health and Student Support Services. He previously served as a School Social Worker and Program Consultant in the San Francisco Unified School District, and has consulted in a number of other school districts. He has a strong interest in school dropout prevention and published his first book in 2020 titled: The Dropout Prevention Specialist Workbook. With a background in both mental health and education, he has tried to bridge and bring the best of these perspectives into the effective delivery of services for children and youth in public education settings. (hblonsky@earthlink.net)

James Wogan is a school administrator and School Social Worker known for innovation and collaboration in support of youth mental health and equity. James currently serves as the Assistant Director of Student Services in the Mt. Diablo Unified School District. He previously served as the Director of Wellness Centers in the Acalanes Unified School District and as Manager of Student Services in the Berkeley Unified School District. James began his career in education in the San Francisco Unified School District. In each of these positions James has developed expanded learning partnerships and fieldwork placements for preparing counseling and school social work candidates to take their place in education. (jameswogan3000@gmail.com)

Preface

This publication came about with the thought of updating the Student Success Team manuals developed in 1998 and 2000 by the California Dropout Prevention Network which was the umbrella organization overseeing the California Dropout Prevention Program that began in 1986 (Senate Bill 65: Pupil Motivation and Maintenance Program).

The Student Success Team (SST) process was seen as a significant "best practice" for the 350 schools enrolled in this program. This best practice has mushroomed both within California and throughout the country. Although there was some mention in the previous SST manuals of what might come prior to convening an SST, the information was limited and lacked specificity. As our own practice in the schools has shown, the SST process is a component part of a larger system of supports for students that involves a number of school-based team structures as described in this publication.

Acknowledgements are recognized to Marci Radius and Pat Lesniak, who worked for the California Special Education Reform Network in the 80's and may have been the first to conceptualize and implement the SST process (previously referred to as the Student Study Team) in schools as a way of organizing services and supporting student success prior to referring them for a formal assessment for consideration of Special Education. As has been shown through practice, the SST process can be successful with students presenting a wide range of issues. The collaborative problem-solving process, brought about by joining the various partners, including the parent/guardian and student, can be a very powerful experience that can lead to improved outcomes in many areas.

The SST volumes published in 1998 and 2000 were developed by six co-authors. They include: Steve Berta, Howard Blonsky, Vicki Butler, Bill Deeb, Marco Orlando and Andy Stetkevich. As you can see, two of the original co-authors have joined together once again, along with the assistance and expertise of James Wogan, to bring an expanded description of a comprehensive student support system. Some of the material in the SST section of this manual has been extracted from the original publication.

The goal of this manual is to help schools to identify and address barriers and obstacles that get in the way of student learning success. We have tried to make this a practical guide with descriptions, frequently asked questions, role descriptions, tips and forms, those which can be copied and modified locally. For any school that has embarked on strengthening their student support services, we sincerely hope this publication is valuable to you, your team members, and ultimately, to the students you serve.

Introduction and Overview

As we put this book together, we realized how overwhelming it can be to create a student support system at a school site. Our schools are literally a reflection of the larger society. Students come to our schools each day and present their struggles and their needs for all to see. We have truant and medically fragile students, we have students battling depression and emotional issues, we have students who are unmotivated, and students who are academically behind. These struggles and needs get in the way of their success in a school setting and can be very difficult to address. With this realization, we saw the importance of starting our book with an understanding of the big picture of student support. How do we go about trying to understand and address these complex issues with the limited resources available to us? How do we build an educational system with sufficient supports to keep students in school with the goal of graduation from high school?

Most successful schools do this by weaving together a positive school culture and climate, joined together with a relevant curriculum, committed teachers and staff, and a range of opportunities, services, and supports needed to make a positive difference in the lives of all of its students. Building a student support system to address these issues is the focus of this publication.

There are three **Core** areas that need to be addressed with our student support systems:

* **Attendance:** This is where it starts. Nothing happens if the student is not in school. Not only do they miss the instruction, but they miss the socialization with their peers, clubs and school activities, and other important relationships. Almost always, truancy is a "red flag" that indicates there is a need to look further to determine what is getting in the way of regular school attendance. When we look under the surface, we often find a complexity of reasons and stressors that are fueling the problem, and these reasons and stressors are what need to be addressed.

- **Behavior and Ways of Thinking:** This relates to how students view their school experience, and their behavior when they are at school. Externalized negative behavior tends to receive more attention, but we must also remember that students with internalized (e.g., sad, withdrawn) struggles also need to be identified and supported. Much like attendance, we must try to understand what the behavior is telling us. At times, reframing the behavior through a new lens, may give us some clues to help us understand how to work with each student.

- **Academics:** Our primary goal is to educate our students and prepare them to be the best version of themselves that they can be, and to help prepare them for adulthood. In our increasingly complex world, we need to look holistically in order to evaluate those things that might get in the way of academic and personal success.

Therefore, all of the supportive structures and services presented in this book come down to just three things:

- Getting our students to school.
- Getting them ready to learn.
- Supporting their learning.

The Four Major Steps:
There are four steps that are crucial to building a successful student support system and they will be presented throughout this publication. Every school's system to support and assist students might look a little different, but every successful system must have these four steps.

1. **Early identification:** The earlier we can identify the challenges that a student is facing, the earlier we can bring appropriate services to that student. But our experience has told us that an unaddressed problem will likely become more serious and, thus, much more difficult to address. Schools must have a process in place that will quickly identify the problems of poor attendance, inappropriate behavior and ways of thinking, and poor academic performance. This first step must be easy and quick because nothing can happen until the problem is identified.

2. **Assessment:** The identified issue is almost always a "red flag" that something is getting in the way of the student's success. This assessment step is to help us understand the root of the problem, often referred to as "peeling the onion down to the core". This step can be much more time consuming. Insight and understanding of the core issue(s) can often be gained from: Talking with the student directly, talking with the parent/guardian, reviewing the cum folder and other school records, talking with staff who know the student and, at times, a visit to the student's home. These steps, and others, can help us to understand what might be inviting the problem that is getting in the way of success. A key component of the assessment step is

to remain culturally sensitive to the information that is gathered, and its potential implications. In our experience, looking for where and how the student is already finding success in their lives, can and should be built upon as it has already been culturally accepted by the student and the family.

3. **Developing a Plan:** After the assessment, a plan must be developed and the resources must be mobilized to address the issues. The supportive services can be found in many forms and are often referred to as the "broad range of interventions". These support services can be found in many places. They can be found and implemented in the classroom setting; they can be found and implemented in the opportunities, services and supports in the larger school environment; they can be found in the home; and, lastly, they can be found within the services and resources of the larger community.

4. **Follow-up:** The final stage is to monitor the effectiveness of the plan and to see whether it is doing what was intended. The follow-up step allows the team to make modifications and to implement other accommodations as needed. It is important that the follow-up occurs in a timely manner. Depending on the situation, a follow-up can happen in a few days or a few weeks after the development of the initial action/intervention plan. The follow-up should occur even if the student is doing well. It can be very powerful for the student to be given positive feedback on a job well done.

School-Based Student Support Structures and the Multi-Level Identification and Intervention Process

Multi-Tiered System of Support

All of the school-based team structures described in this manual utilize a Multi-Tiered System of Support (MTSS) to conceptualize which level of intervention is needed for a particular student. School teams benefit from using a Multi-Tiered System of Support (MTSS) as a framework for mapping the resources available within the school and the larger community, and identifying service and program gaps within the school community. This helps teams to understand which gaps need to be filled, whether in the school, the district, or in the larger community. All three levels of intervention and support can help to increase students' social, emotional and behavioral health, thereby leading to improved personal and academic outcomes.

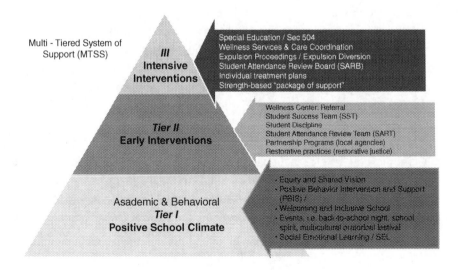

DOI: 10.4324/9781003240266-1

Positive Behavior Interventions and Supports (PBIS) provides a school-wide framework for achieving these outcomes. The PBIS is a decision-making framework that guides the selection, integration, and implementation of the best evidence-based academic and behavioral practices for improving school climate and behavior outcomes.

The three tiers of support typically include:

Tier I: Tier I involves the entire school community, the culture and climate of the school, and a welcoming school environment that is inclusive for students and families from diverse backgrounds and lifestyles. This tier includes developing positive relationships between students, staff and families of the students. This is the first place to implement Positive Behavior Interventions and Supports (PBIS), which is composed of four elements: 1) Staff, 2) Students, 3) Parents and Guardians and 4) The School Environment. A common misconception of MTSS is that there is no point in implementing Tier III if Tier I and II are not already in place. Research in Trauma Informed Practices [1] demonstrates that many students arrive at school already in need of intensive (Tier III) support services. Principals and educational leaders share the belief that Tier I, II and III must be implemented concurrently. School climate (PBIS, Tier I) can be disrupted by students with unmet behavioral-health needs. Included in Tier I are classroom community-building strategies to create a supportive and culturally sensitive classroom with students working together and getting to know one another.

Improving student academic and behavior outcomes is about ensuring that all students have access to the most effective and accurately implemented instructional and behavioral practices and interventions possible. As educators, these are the things we have some control over and that are within our power to implement.

Tier II: Tier II involves providing interventions based on an evaluation of each student's needs, and monitoring the response to the interventions, supports and services provided. This is similar to what is commonly known as Response to Intervention (RTI). We have the ability to develop and implement various opportunities, services and supports, to change what is taught, how it is taught, and the climate in which it is taught. *The general goal of Tier II is to intervene early when problems arise in order to prevent them from becoming chronic and severe.*

Tier III: The goal of Tier III is to provide specialized services and supports to students with chronic and severe challenges that impede access to instruction and academic success. Tier III interventions provide expanded learning partnerships that include higher level programs and resources available in the school, the district, and through linkages to the broader community (e.g., wrap around services, trauma informed services, intensive "case" management, as well as specialized classes and programs within the regular education environment).

Per the provisions of "search and serve", students with illnesses and/or disabilities are identified and can be served via the Individualized Education Program (IEP) process and Section 504 of the Rehabilitation Act of 1973.

Opportunities, Services and Supports

Opportunities: Research has shown that when young people are given an **opportunity** to contribute to their school community, it has the effect of improving their own self-esteem, and increasing their bond with the school. Leadership roles in student government, serving as a peer helper, as a member of a gardening program, a school beautification project, or those students who participate in collecting turkeys and other needed supplies for deserving families at the holidays are leadership opportunities to contribute. (Opportunities are a good example of a Tier I Universal Interventions).

Services are defined as those interventions that are available either based at the school, or linked to the school through a Memorandums of Understanding (MOU's), or other such defined relationships. These include health and mental health services available in a Wellness Center that offer individual or group counseling/therapy, health education and assistance with safe sex practices. Other services provided in the school might include learning labs, tutoring, opportunity programs and classes, case management services, newcomer assistance, access to food banks and clothes closets, assistance with enrollment in state sponsored health plans, as well as specialized programs and services within the community.

We must be continually aware that the opportunities, services and/or supports that we offer to students must be viewed through a cultural lens. We must make sure that the services and/or the service agencies, with which we try to engage our students and their families, are culturally sensitive, inclusive of language and ethnic differences in their practices, and are appreciative and respectful of the educational background, customs and mores, and lifestyle differences of those they are dealing with.

(These services can be considered as Tier II, however some can also be Tier 1, such as tutoring that is offered to all students who might benefit from them).

Supports are those programs and services within the school environment that assist students in various ways such as small group remediation, credit recovery options, mentoring, restorative justice practices, independent study contracts, make-up classes, re-entry programs, ethnic identity clubs and activities, leadership opportunities, special interest clubs, recognition for improved grades, attendance and behavior. (Some of these may be considered Tier III interventions, although some of these can transcend all three tiers).

To the extent that a school has many opportunities, services and supports in place, a greater number of students and their parents/guardians are likely to bond with the school, and provide the student support teams a variety of options to draw upon for Action/Intervention Planning.

> A school can create a "coherent" environment, a climate, more potent than any single influence—teachers, class, family, neighborhood—so potent that for at least six hours a day it can override almost everything else in the lives of children.
>
> [2]

Student Support Team Structures and the Filtering/Funneling Process

Years of experience have taught us that having team structures in a school for the delivery of supports and services can significantly improve school climate and student achievement. While the implementation of these teams might look somewhat different school by school, they all share a vision of success for each student. Amid rapidly changing technology and life circumstances, it is essential that every school should have in place a student support team structure or structures. As has been said, every school should regularly take a look at how effectively their student support teams are accomplishing what they were intended to do.

The extent to which teachers and other staff members collaborate with each other often depends on the collaborative structures and positive climate in the school setting for staff members. Effective leaders anticipate and normalize disagreement on how best to utilize limited resources and include the perspective of stakeholders from diverse backgrounds. In the midst of rapidly changing technology and shifting norms, student support teams provide a platform for reflection on the way in which each stakeholder group is utilized in the school. Student support teams assist student services administrators in examining data and identifying areas for ongoing professional development and training, as well as developing new programs and services or modifying current ones. Periodically, the duties of student services personnel might need to be realigned within job descriptions to meet current conditions. Systemic change such as this is most telling when incorporated into the shared vision and goals set forth by the superintendent and board of education.

Keep in mind that student support team structures can quickly become overwhelmed by the number of students being referred or identified via school data systems, if there are no progressive levels of intervention. Both school staff members and students can benefit from a "filtering/funneling" process at the school. If the needs of the student can be addressed at the first or second level, there will be fewer students identified and referred for higher-level services.

There is a finite pool of resources available to our schools, and we have to use them as wisely as possible. A "filtering/funneling" process helps in this regard.

Early Identification and Intervention are Powerful Keys to Success

Level I: The Classroom

The first level for observation and intervention is most often in the classroom environment. The unique relationship between student and teacher can have a profound influence not only on the academic growth of the student but also on their psychological and social growth as well. Classroom teachers differentiate for all students to the extent possible, and they are the ones who can modify instructional strategies and provide accommodations based on the learning style and needs of each child. Teachers are encouraged to utilize various lists and manuals of possible interventions that are widely available, one of which is mentioned in the next Chapter. These resources should be available at each school site providing suggestions to address specific areas of concern exhibited in the classroom setting.

Level II: Grade Level (or Subject Alike) Teacher Teams

Prior to referring a student to the next level of assistance, teachers are expected to discuss their concerns about a particular student with other grade-level or subject alike teachers. A current teacher may also reach out to a prior teacher or counselor who might be able to provide a particular strategy, motivator, or reinforcement(s) that the current teacher can utilize. This sharing allows for input from multiple perspectives and reinforces teamwork that is important to have at every level in the school. When school staff are working as a team the entire culture and climate of the school will improve.

In a middle school where one of the authors previously served as a member of the student support team, the counselor(s), school social worker, school psychologist, and the mental health support staff would meet regularly with the teachers from each grade level to discuss and strategize their combined efforts with each student. Everyone's perspective was honored and respected, and a feeling of mutual support grew with each meeting. Collaborative discussions can lead to shared strategies, mentorships, instructional modifications, rewards, naming a "buddy" for a student, and other actions/interventions that might evolve through these discussions.

A question that invariably arises is when does/can a team meeting like this happen? In the same middle school described above, the team meetings were held before school started in the morning on a rotational schedule. One week the sixth grade, the next week the seventh, and the third week the eighth, and then the rotation would start over again. At the high school level, collaborative meetings can be held by grade level, subject alike, or possibly a "school within a school family", and can be scheduled on alternate weeks when another meeting is not scheduled.

In these discussions, the teachers can share strategies about a particular student of concern. Early morning, before school starts, seems to work best, unless there is a common planning time. Meeting by grade levels and multiple subjects removes the isolation of subject alike clustered meetings.

Once these collaborative meetings become routine, teachers report the discussions can be beneficial for the students and they increase their own sense of teamwork.

When the efforts at Levels I and II are not effective enough, the teacher or a representative of the grade level team should complete a Request for Assistance Form (Please see sample in the Appendix) and submit it to the coordinator/facilitator of the Care Team for placement on the agenda at an upcoming meeting.

Level III. The School Coordinated Care Team (SCCT)

The Care Team, much like the Student Success Team, is a problem-solving and coordinating structure where all of the support personnel at the school, both those who are based at the school, as well as itinerant personnel assigned to the school, come together every week, or at least every other week, to discuss new students of concern, and to monitor the plans of students who have come before the team before. The Care Team also works to coordinate the efforts of all of the service providers to avoid duplication of effort, and to look at patterns and trends in the student body and the school community that may require systemic intervention.

Unlike the Student Success Team and the School Attendance Review Team, the Care Team does not involve students and their parent(s)/guardian(s), and participation is limited to those student support personnel providers, either employed by a school district, or from community agencies that are based at, or linked to, the school.

Therefore, the Care Team reviews multiple students in each meeting. (Please see sample SCCT agenda in the Appendix).

In planning their action items, the following two team structures can be utilized. A complete description of these teams is located in the Chapters on the Student Success Team and the Student Attendance Review Team.

Student Success Team (SST) Process

The SST is a strength-based problem-solving structure that works with the significant people in the life of the student to build and implement a plan of success.

The goal of the SST is to seek positive solutions for maximizing a student's potential. The SST philosophy is based on the belief that the school, home and community need to work together to assist the student with obstacles that become evident in the school setting. The SST process seeks: to set a course for assisting the student, to build a network of support, to implement a variety of interventions/actions, and to monitor the results.

Most of the time the Care Team recommends an SST meeting when they believe it would be helpful to bring together all of the significant people in the life of the student for discussion and problem-solving.

The Student Attendance Review Team (SART)

Every school should have a Student Attendance Review Team (SART) to follow the progress of students whose attendance patterns are of concern. Much like the Care Team and the SST, the SART works to understand and address what underlies the poor attendance and what works to address the issues identified with any or all of the resources they have at their disposal.

The SART is also responsible to promote positive attendance practices and reinforcements in the school, such as a listing of students with perfect or improved attendance, prizes for the classroom(s) with the best attendance, and other means of recognition. Just like the Care Team, the SART is responsible to identify patterns of systemic issues that might be contributing to poor attendance and dropouts from the school/district.

The "Filtering/Funneling" Process as a Best Practice

It is important to note that although a "funneling/filtering" process is considered a best practice, certain situations require more immediate attention and it might be necessary to take multiple steps concurrently. Starting with classroom interventions (Level I), and having groups of teachers meet to discuss their students (Level II), are good ideas, and should be followed as much as possible.

Integration of Student Support Teams into the Fabric of the School

As student support teams are integrated into the fabric of school communities, growing pains are inherent to systemic changes and more traditional ways of working. Student support teams are highly effective and efficient once they are up and running.

School-based student service providers often encounter gaps between support services that are available versus the needs of their students. In order to address unmet needs, team members need to think "out of the box" in finding ways to develop new programs and services, or modifying existing services and programs.

Even the most efficient and well-trained teams must reflect on school-wide practices and policies to determine if any are contributing factors to the lack of student success. Schools need to use a continuous cycle of inquiry and improvement to meet changing student needs.

Drawing Strength from Diversity

The United States is made up of, and continues to draw its strength from, the rich diversity of its people. The picture of America is an ever-changing mosaic. Our task is to appreciate the value and richness of the individual pieces and how they contribute to and enhance the beauty of the whole work of art.

Within the framework of the student support structures, working with students and parents of diverse ethnic or cultural backgrounds, can pose challenges to the kind of communication necessary to achieve success. Potential barriers to communication can include the diversity of cultures, belief systems, customs, values, and languages of the students and their caregivers. However, we must also be cognizant of the lived experiences and belief systems of the school staff who represent the other side of the communication process. If there is a disconnect in this two-way communication, it can negatively affect the collaborative and joining process between the parties. Any and all of these factors can pose challenges to the support team structures and processes. They must be acknowledged and addressed. When in doubt, we feel the key is to ask and to listen, in order to learn what is appropriate in each individual circumstance.

Before parents/guardians feel comfortable sharing their concerns and observations about their student, it is necessary to establish rapport and a trusting relationship with them. In order to do this, school personnel will need to invest additional time in getting to know the family in the context of their cultural or ethnic background. This is particularly true of parents/guardians who do not speak English. Offering the services of a trained interpreter/translator who speaks English, can help to facilitate communication with the family. Staff/team members need to keep in mind that there is a great deal of variation among families in the same cultural group. Factors such as educational background, length of time in the United States, socioeconomic status, religion, and the size of the cultural community can account for individual differences. When in doubt, or not, ask questions.

In both the Student Success Team (SST) process and the School Attendance Review Team (SART) conferences with parents/guardians, pre-meeting preparations are essential. For example, it may be necessary to provide forms in the home language of the parents/guardians, to provide interpreters for the meeting itself, and to include appropriate site and community personnel who can contribute to successful communication and collaboration, factors extremely necessary for the benefit of the student. If one of these meetings is multi-lingual, additional time will most often be necessary to allow for this accommodation.

Remember, we all have the same goal in mind: for the student(s) to be successful. Effective communication with all people begins and ends with respect.

References

1   Burke-Harris, Nadine M.D., *Trauma Informed Practices that Work*, https://www.edutopia.org/video/3-trauma-informed-practices-backed-science, October 16, 2020.
2   Edmonds, Ron, *The School Achievement of Minority Children*, Mahwah, New Jersey, Lawrence Erlbaum Associates, Inc., 1986.

2 | The School Coordinated Care Team (SCCT)

We particularly like referring to the SCCT as the Care Team because it implies caring for the students, the reasons we are all doing this kind of work.

What is a Coordinated Care Team and Why do We Need One at Our School?

The School Coordinated Care Team (hereafter "Care Team") is a structure that saves staff time by bringing together the student support staff on a regular basis. The Care Team often obviates the need for each staff member to call, email, or individually to discuss one student at a time. The team brings together the student support staff assigned to the school, both those who are based at the school, as well as those who work at the school on a part time "itinerant" basis (e.g., school psychologist, speech and language clinician, school nurse).

Unlike the Student Success Team and the School Attendance Review Team, the Care Team does not meet with the parents/guardians of the student, because multiple students, and their needs, are addressed in each meeting. If one of the action items from the Care Team is for a member of the team to meet with the parent or guardian, that can be listed as part of an action/intervention plan.

The Care Team also serves to coordinate the resources and services of the school, those available in the district, and the school-based and school-linked services and programs of the greater community which support and contribute to the work of the Care Team. It helps to avoid the duplication of effort from programs and service providers or working at cross purposes. The Care Team also looks for trends/patterns of the issues brought before the team in individual students, along with other data available to the school that can be used for identification of a particular student or group of students.

DOI: 10.4324/9781003240266-2

The Team may recommend the need for new programs or services to address these trends/patterns as they are manifested in the student population.

> By meeting as a team, the Care Team prevents people from working in isolation. Plans are made on behalf of student(s) with the input and perspective of others from various disciplines. In this way the Care Team increases efficiency, and reduces costs that would be incurred from individuals working on their own.

The Care Team has the following purposes

1. To provide the development and coordination of plans on behalf of multiple students at each meeting, and provide follow-up and oversight of plans developed at previous meetings.
2. To maintain a record of the Action Plans for each student, along with a record of the follow-up meeting dates that have been determined.
3. To maintain a record of the signed Oath of Confidentiality of each member of Care Team.
4. To ensure that people are not working at cross purposes or duplicating efforts.
5. To make sure that the perspective and expertise of various disciplines and individuals are heard, respected and considered.
6. To list the dates of important meetings, such as scheduled SST's, on the Care Team agenda, so that everyone on the team is aware of them, and can decide whether they should attend.
7. To consider any patterns or trends reflected in the referred population, as well as the general school population, that might need systemic actions/interventions. Disaggregating and interpreting the data generated at the school, (e.g., test scores of various groups, students receiving D's and F's, and English language learners) can provide useful insights about the success, or lack of same, of various populations in the school. This should lead to a discussion about the need for developing new programs, services and resources, or making modifications to existing programs.

Many schools across the United States have some forum of what we have described as a School Coordinated Care Team (SCCT) or Care Team. Some of the names these teams have been given are: Student Assistance Program (SAP), Coordination of Services Team (COST), Multidisciplinary Team (MDT), or the Student Intervention Team (SIP). As stated above, we like to use the term, the Care Team, short for School Coordinated Care Team, in that it implies caring for the students.

> The Care Team meeting, unlike the Student Success Team (SST) process, or Student Attendance Review Team conferences, do not include the student and his/her caregivers. Therefore, the Care Team discusses many students, along with program coordination and development issues in each meeting.

When Can/Does Our Coordinated Care Team Meet? We Are All So Busy Already

It is expected that the Care Team will meet at a regularly scheduled time each week, or at least bi-weekly. It is hoped that an entire morning is reserved for Care Team and Student Success Team (SST) meetings. Hopefully, the schedules of itinerant personnel have been coordinated at the district level so that they can join with the other student support personnel stationed at the site, so that they can all be at the school for this important regular meeting.

A typical morning schedule might look something like the following: The Care Team meeting would take place from 8:00 AM until 9:30. Following the Care Team meeting, there will be two to four SST meetings held, each one lasting forty-five minutes to one hour. Of course, other important meetings, including SST's, are conducted at other times during the week. When to hold these important meetings will differ from school to school. While some student service personnel may leave after the Care Team meeting, others may choose to stay and attend one or more SST meetings, especially if they are familiar with the student, are providing services to the student, or might become involved in providing services to the student.

It does require a great deal of flexibility by each member of the team to dedicate the necessary time to participate in Care Team meetings. It is believed that the time spent is very worthwhile, and will prove useful to students, staff and the school as a whole. We hope that all Care Team participants will make a commitment to regularly attend these meetings, and that they have the full support of the administration to make this commitment.

Who will Be on Our Coordinated Care Team?

The number and roles of the members of the Care Team who will serve as regular members are listed below. These will vary from school to school:

* Principal, Assistant Principal, or designee.
* Care Team facilitator.
* Teachers: Referring teacher(s) whenever possible, or a person representing the input of the others teacher(s) of the student.
* School social worker.
* Guidance counselor(s).
* School nurse.
* Attendance specialist.
* Dropout prevention specialist (DPS).
* Wellness center staff.

* Special Education representative.
* Mental health staff.
* Speech and Language clinician.
* Parent liaison.
* After school program staff.
* School-based or school-linked mental health service provider(s).
* A representative from City/County or community-based agencies with whom the school or district has formed partnerships.
* Others at the school who can make a contribution to the discussion.

Who is in Charge of the Coordinated Care Team?

There are certain roles that must be assumed by a member or members of the team, but these roles are/can be fluid, and unless one of these roles is clearly defined in an individual's job description, they can be rotated from one person to another at various points in time, such as at the end of a quarter or a semester.

The pre-meeting **coordinator** and meeting **facilitator** can be the same person, or two people who play different roles in making the Care Team a success. These individuals are not necessarily called "leaders", but rather those who work to ensure the smooth running of this important process. The coordinator/facilitator functions are obviously very important, and those who assume these roles should have the trust of the members of the team.

What are the Care Team's Roles and Responsibilities?

A member of the team is selected to receive the Request for Assistance Forms and to serve as the **coordinator** of the pre-meeting process, and a **facilitator** of the actual Care Team meeting.

Pre-meeting coordinator

* Schedules the meeting place, time and date, and informs all members of these.
* Prepares the agenda that includes new students, follow-up students, important meetings scheduled (such as SST's), along with program coordination and development issues to be discussed.
* Distributes the agenda to the Care Team at least two days in advance of the meeting.
* Ensures that all relevant records and documentation will be at the meeting table.

Facilitator

* Facilitates the meeting, moving the discussion along in a respectful way.
* Ensures the agenda is covered in a timely manner.

* Ensures that all ideas are considered before formalizing the Care/Action Plan.
* Ensures that the administration and faculty are kept informed of Care Team activities.

The facilitator of the meeting is much like an orchestra leader. S/he guides the discussion, sets a respectful and task-oriented tone, and listens to all perspectives and ideas. S/he works with the timekeeper to keep each discussion succinct and moving along, as there are typically many students to be discussed.

(A fuller description of the roles and skills in facilitation are found in Chapter 5 on Facilitation.)

Recorder

* Brings a record keeping system to each meeting, including the school calendar.
* Ensures that an Oath of Confidentiality is signed by each member of the team, and kept with other Care Team material.
* Keeps an attendance record of the key members of the team.
* Maintains records on all students brought before the team.
* Records salient information on the Action Plan document for each student.
* Provides a verbal summary of decisions to ensure the accuracy of notes.
* Notifies the coordinator of students to be scheduled for a follow-up meeting.

Timekeeper

* Assists the facilitator in starting and ending on time.
* Keeps the meeting on schedule once members have determined time allocations.

Team members

* Arrive on time.
* Notify the facilitator if absence or late arrival is anticipated.
* Are prepared with relevant materials if presenting any part of the discussion about a particular student.
* Help the team to stay on focus.
* Participate in "brainstorming", providing suggestions and resources for every student discussed.

When a Student of Concern is Presented for Discussion Before the Care Team, What is Expected to be Brought to the Meeting Table?

Having the right documentation and materials at the meeting table will avoid having to search for information later that would have helped to know the student better if this information had been provided at the time of the meeting. These include:

* The Request for Assistance form.
* The cumulative (cum) folder (The person who refers the student to the team, or the guidance counselor, should have reviewed the "cum" folder and be able to highlight relevant information (e.g., previous test data, past school history, health/ medical issues, contacts with the family).
* A Teacher Input Form from each of the student's current teachers.
* Recent report card, scholarship record, attendance record, and any record of disciplinary actions.
* At the elementary level, recent work samples and/or in-class assignments.

Presentation of a Student for Discussion to the Care Team

The presenter should be prepared to discuss in the following order:

* The strengths of the student.
* Significant background information.
* What has already been attempted and what the results have been.
* Current issues and concerns.
* Ideas and/or direction of how to proceed from this point forward.

If the necessary material and documentation is presented to the Care Team in the manner suggested, the discussion of each student should not take more than 10–12 minutes, often less for follow-ups. If the presentation of the student is done in a complete and concise way, the chance for the development of a complete and potentially effective plan will be enhanced.

(A typical CARE Team meeting would take about 1½ hours).

Does the Coordinated Care Team Structure Function the Same Way at the Elementary, Middle or High School Levels?

Essentially yes, but with some minor differences as follows. At the elementary level, it may be the referring teacher who presents the student for discussion, or they may do this in partnership with a peer teacher liaison who is a core member of the school's Care Team.

At the middle school level, it is assumed that teachers have regularly scheduled grade level or "academic family" meetings, and this team has "brainstormed" ideas, and tried various interventions on behalf of the student. When a middle school student is presented to the Care Team for discussion, a representative of the teacher(s) team, or the counselor who has met with the student and his/her teachers, will present the student to the other members of the Care Team. Both at the elementary and middle school levels, when a Care Team meeting is being held during the school day, it is important that coverage of the teacher's classroom be provided for them to attend the discussion of a particular student. Hopefully, the administration will be supportive of this, and do whatever they can to make the class coverage possible for a relatively short period of time. As previously stated, some middle schools will schedule a discussion of students' one grade level at a time, such as the sixth grade team one week, the seventh grade team the next week, and the eighth grade team the following week. In order for the entire grade level team to be present, the meeting should be held before school starts. In this model, both new students and students for follow-up discussion for that grade level would be the first items on the agenda. The other members of the Care Team can continue with the discussion once the classroom teachers have gone to their respective classrooms.

At the high school level, it is very difficult to get of all of the student's teachers to the table at one time, and most often they do not meet in grade level teams. To accommodate this difference, the counselor of the student would present the concern(s) about the student to the team, making sure that they have the written input for each of the students' teachers. (See the sample Teacher Input Form in the Appendix.)

What Would a Typical Care Team Agenda Look Like?

* Usually, the first item on the agenda is a discussion of individual students who have not been discussed before the team previously. This number may be anywhere from two to six or seven.
* The second item on the agenda would be a listing of students who were previously discussed before the team, and who already have a School Coordinated Services Plan. The purpose of these discussions is to follow up the progress of the original plan, and to make any necessary changes to the plan, as indicated. Setting a date for subsequent review/follow-ups is decided and recorded.
* The next item on the agenda would be a listing of the SST meetings and SART conferences that are scheduled, so that members of the team who plan to attend these meetings can put the information on their calendars.
* Following a listing of SSTs and other important meetings and discussions that are scheduled, any program and/or coordination issues can be discussed. This could include a discussion of a current program or service, or a program or service need based on identified trends/patterns in the student body. This information can be joined with other data available at/to the school by disaggregating the academic, attendance and behavioral data. Based on these discussions, the team might decide to develop a proposal and/or apply for a grant, modify a current program or structure in the school, and/or "brainstorm" ideas on how to address what has been learned.

- The last item on the agenda can list any issues that members of the team want to be placed on the agenda for the next meeting. (A sample of a Care Team agenda can be found in the Appendix.)

The Oath of Confidentiality

Each member of the Care Team is asked to sign an Oath of Confidentiality. By having everyone sign an Oath of Confidentiality, individuals are stating, under penalty of law, they will not divulge sensitive information about the student and his/her family beyond the members of the Care Team. The signed Oath (see sample in the SCCT Appendix) will be kept at the beginning of the Care Team binder along with the Care/Action Plan documents for individual students. (This can also be done virtually, but an old-fashioned binder can be a good place to start.)

Knowledge of Resources

It is also important for all members who serve on one or more teams to be knowledgeable about how to access the services and resources of the school, the school district, and of the broader community. These would typically include a contact person's name, the services provided, any important eligibility requirements, the time and days the services are available, the potential duration of the services offered, and any other important information. There might be a defined relationship or a Memorandum of Understanding (MOU) with the school, and hopefully some of this information would be provided in those documents.

It is a good idea for the team to undertake a "mapping" of the resources of the community, and a list developed for members of the Care Team to draw upon when deciding on a referral or particular intervention that goes beyond the school boundaries. By the same token, the Care Team should also have a list of the opportunities, services and supports offered within the school or the larger school district.

Brainstorming and the Development of a Plan of Action/ Intervention

After being presented with the referral and documentation, members of the team "brainstorm" the possible next steps, what the Action/Intervention Plan might contain. The Action Plan could take a variety of tracks such as: Schedule a Student Success Team meeting, providing suggestions to the student's teachers or caregivers, a change of program, a home visit, a meeting with one or more of the student's teachers with the student and caregiver (not a formal SST), credit recovery options that will be offered to the student, a referral to the Student Attendance Review Team, (SART), mental health services, a mentor, or a leadership opportunity.

The Care Team decides on the package of interventions/services, and decides to monitor them, or they can refer the student to another one of the team structures. For each student discussed, a School Coordinated Services Plan will be completed and a copy kept in the Care Team binder. A copy is also provided to each member of the team who has responsibilities defined in the plan, along with the date by which the action is to occur, and a defined date to bring the student back for follow-up review. (There are many versions of a form such as this, certainly creating one to fit your school is strongly suggested. Please see sample Care Team Summary/Action Plan document in the Appendix.)

It is important to emphasize again that the Care Team will only be successful if the time is watched carefully. If the discussion does not move along in the manner suggested, other needy students will be deprived of a discussion and service planning on their behalf.

What types of Interventions/Accommodations/Modifications are Typically Developed by the Care Team?

Whether at the Care Team, in an SST meeting, or in a School Attendance Review Team conference, the following areas for intervention, often referred to as the "Broad Range of Interventions", should be considered:

* Classroom assistance/modifications/accommodations.
* Opportunities, services and supports available at the larger school, but not necessarily in each classroom (i.e., tutoring, mentoring, and after school programs).
* Assistance from/with the family.
* Utilization of community-based services, programs and resources.

(The broad range of interventions is repeated a number of places in the manual with various examples to emphasize its importance).

The following more fully describes the "broad range of interventions" that can and should be considered at a Care Team meeting, in a Student Success Team meeting, in a Student Attendance Review Team conference, or in the "case management" phase of the work:

a. The classroom

Teachers have a difficult job. Classroom teachers are crucial collaborative partners with the Care Team. It is not uncommon for a teacher to have ten or more students in their classroom who need one form of assistance or another, or a package of services needed/developed on their behalf.

Teachers can and do have an incredible influence on their students. One quote from a gifted teacher by the name of Hiam Ginott [1] follows:

> I have come to the frightening conclusion
> I am the decisive element in the classroom.
> It is my personal approach that creates the climate.
> It is my daily mood that makes the weather.
> As a teacher I possess tremendous power to make a child's life miserable or joyous.
> I can humiliate or humor, hurt or heal.
> In all situations, it is my response that decides whether a crisis will be escalated or de-escalated, and a child humanized or de-humanized.

Children's needs, learning styles, trigger points, and motivators are so diverse that no single teacher can provide all of the strategies or answers. The spirit of the team structures is a collaborative one in which members of the team are encouraged to share ideas and strategies with one another. It is useful if the team you are serving on maintains a "library" of resources that have worked in the past. One such document is the Pre-Referral Intervention Manual: The Most Common Learning and Behavior Problems Encountered in the Classroom.[2] With regard to classroom interventions, if these are part of the Care/Action Plan, it might be a good idea for a peer teacher, if one is a member of the team, to be the one who assumes the responsibility to work with the classroom teacher on any suggested instructional modifications or strategies.

b. The larger school environment

To the extent the school has developed a range of opportunities, services and supports, as discussed in the introductory chapter, within the school environment, the Care Team has a variety of school wide resources to draw upon for the Care/Action Planning.

Members of the Care Team should be familiar with such details regarding who the contact person is for each program or activity, any special eligibility requirements, the time, place and duration of the service or program to which the student is being referred. The student should be encouraged to seek out this information for themselves (empowerment), but members of the Care Team should be willing to fill in any details that had been missed by the student. A member of the Care Team should check in with the student after a reasonable period of time to see if the student has made the connection to the campus service or program recommended. The positive relations that are developed between staff members and the student, the range of choices made available to the student to develop interests and skills in art, music, athletics and other interests can go a long way in developing or reinforcing self-esteem and keeping students coming to school. The relationship between the Care Team member and the student is very important in using encouragement and advocacy to "glue" together various needs and services.

c. In/with the home

The stressors within the family can be part of the problem, and the strengths of the family can be part of the solution. Stressors might include housing, the need to develop employment related skills, health care, respite, food and clothing deficiencies, and the need for more education. Strengths include those things that caregivers can do to support the students learning, such as regular communication with the school, requiring daily or weekly progress reports, arranging for a time and place for the student to do homework and reading, taking the student for a medical exam, participation in family therapy, spending more quality time with the student, or implementing rewards and consequences. If possible, it is recommended that a member of the team (e.g., counselor, social worker, parent liaison) discuss the concerns with the parent(s)/guardian(s) prior to the Care Team, in order to hear their perspective, along with their thoughts/suggestions that can be shared at the meeting.

The representative of the Care Team might encounter a good deal of resistance to the plan of assistance on the part of the student or caregiver(s), and the worker will have to spend time trying to understand these obstacles and help to overcome them. Here again, the importance of the relationship cannot be overstated. The teamwork effort can have a profoundly positive impact on their youngster, positive changes that can and do occur.

> If you approach others with the thought of compassion, that will automatically reduce fear and allows for openness with other people. It creates a positive, friendly atmosphere. With that attitude, you can approach a relationship in which you, yourself, initially create the possibility of receiving a positive response from the other person. With that attitude, even if the other person is unfriendly or doesn't respond to you in a positive way, then at least you've approached the person with the feeling of openness that gives you the flexibility, and the freedom to change your approach, if needed. That kind of openness at least allows the possibility of having a meaningful conversation with them.
>
> [3]

d. In/with the community

Members of the school-based student support teams should have a good understanding of the range of services, agencies, providers, and programs in the community.

Most communities have service directories provided by the United Way or another reputable umbrella organization. As previously mentioned, it is a good idea for member(s) of the Care Team to do a "mapping" of the programs and resources of the broader community to serve as possible action items for the team to draw upon for intervention planning.

Linking and Gluing the Services Together

Since the School Coordinated Services Plan was developed without the input of the family at the team meeting, a member of the team should reach out and communicate the key plan components to the caregivers, in particular those action items that involve them. Much like the other team structures, involvement with the family as a collaborative partner is the goal.

Often someone is identified as the "point person" or "case (care) manager" who is selected to help "glue" the plan together and monitor its effects.

Some of the best ways to ensure a referral to a particular service agency is to provide the caregiver with the name and the phone number of a particular worker with whom a member of the team has developed a relationship. Another way that a member of the team can help to "cement" the connection between the needs and a particular resource is to invite the service provider and the family to have their first meeting at the school. This is often referred to as "bridging" to services. This approach can be far more effective than simply passing the name and phone number to the student or caregiver(s). Again, this is where the personal relationship can have a significant impact in performing this role.

Monitoring and Follow-Up

When there is follow-up and monitoring the effectiveness of services/intervention plans, and modifications to the plan are made as needed, there is a much better chance that positive change will occur. In terms of equity and disproportionality, effective Care Teams and strong SST practices can often obviate the need for a student being referred for Special Education identification and assessment. Those interventions, actions and modifications decided in good faith at the Care Team, a Student Success Team meeting, or a School Attendance Review Team conference are only as good as the follow-up occurs to ensure the actions agreed upon are implemented. Follow-up is crucial if the plan is to succeed.

1. At the time of the follow-up meeting, the team should decide whether the interventions/ modifications were on the path to success, and whether new or revised actions should be undertaken.
2. The team should also decide whether a particular student should continue to be monitored. Students can continue to be placed on the agenda for follow-up discussion at various intervals at the discretion of the team.

3. The process of "gluing" together the defined needs with the interventions, modifications, strategies, programs and resources is often referred to as "case management". In actuality, the case management process starts much earlier than the follow-up phase (see Chapter 9 on "Case Management"). At times, a/the person who assumes this function is called the "point person", but there might be more than one point person assigned to various components of the plan.

4. If one is serving in the role of the "point person" (or case manager), the person must check back with the Action Plan items and do one or more of the following:

   * Make a phone call to determine if the agreed-upon action has occurred.
   * Chat with the teacher(s), school staff and the student to see whether their assigned responsibilities have been implemented
   * Send a reminder note.
   * Check in at defined intervals with those who have agreed to undertake an action item.
   * Set up a meeting on-site with a service provider to help "bridge" the student/ family to a particular program or agency.

5. Working with students to "own" the plan and to undertake actions on their own behalf is an important part of the follow-up. Students have to feel that they have some control over their own destiny and that we are allies rather than adults having all of the control. The same is true for the students' caregivers as well.

6. If the services/resources that were recommended for the student do not take, we should check whether there was a bureaucratic or systemic issue that contributed to a potential mismatch, or whether the services/resources were not culturally sensitive and aligned with the student and/or family.

7. It is important for the referring person(s) to receive feedback on the Action Plan that was developed as an outcome of the referral. It is also beneficial to involve them, if they were not part of developing the Action Plan, in some ownership of the plan. If the action items involve classroom strategies, modifications and adaptations, it is very important that the classroom teacher be consulted, as they will be crucial to the success of the plan.

SCCT Tip Sheet

Organizational preparation for a Care Team meeting

1. There need to be a designated person (coordinator) and location for the Request for Assistance/Referral Forms to be submitted.

2. There needs to be a system to log in the receipt of these requests.

3.   A designated person should "triage" these Requests for Assistance to ensure completeness and appropriateness before being heard before the Care Team. If needed, they should be returned to the referring source for additional documentation.

4.   There needs to be a designated person to distribute and collect Teacher Input Forms from each teacher of the student (primarily at the secondary level).

5.   An agenda needs to be developed for each Care Team meeting and distributed to each member of the team at least two days in advance of the meeting.

6.   Participants responsible for presenting a student for discussion should be reminded to collect the necessary information and documentation needed for presentation.

The person who assumes the responsibility for organizing the Care Team and making sure that everything is in place for a productive discussion will need to be someone with very good organizational skills and a "collaborative personality".

At the Care Team meeting

1.   All relevant personnel involved in student support services are represented at the Care Team meeting.

2.   A meeting facilitator, recorder and timekeeper are evident at the meeting.

3.   The person who presents the student for discussion is prepared to discuss the history of the student as well as interventions that have been attempted, and what the results have been, current concerns, and the recommendations of the presenter. (The better prepared and complete the presentation is, the more fruitful and time-focused will be the discussion).

4.   The input of all participants in the meeting is solicited during the "brain-storming" phase of the discussion, and each person's contributions are respected.

5.   A range of interventions are discussed that include: 1) the classroom, 2) the opportunities, services, and supports of the school and school district, 3) in/with the home, and 4) the services and resources of the broader community.

6.   A listing of agency partners, and the services and programs they represent, who serve students at the school, is available to the Care Team. In addition, any specific referral criteria, contact person(s), and other relevant information is included.

7.   A written School Coordinated Services Plan is developed before the meeting concludes. The plan includes who is responsible for each action and the deadline for completion.

8.   A date for a follow-up meeting is set. The names of each student scheduled for a follow-up discussion is put back on the agenda at the date determined.

9. A "point person", sometimes called a "case carrier" or "case manager" should be appointed to make sure that the interventions agreed actually happen. This person serves as a "glue person", working to glue the plan together, and to hold those who have agreed to implement various parts of the plan to follow through on their agreed-upon responsibilities.

Service/Program coordination and development discussion guidelines

The team should:

1. Consider patterns/trends of concern observed within the referred student population, as well as within the overall school population.
2. Discuss the need for developing additional services, programs and resources (e.g., support groups, mentoring programs, leadership and service opportunities, additional clubs and activities).
3. Discuss recommendations for instructional and/or curricular changes the better to meet the needs of students.
4. Consider steps needed to be taken toward development and implementation of recommended changes.

SCCT: Key Concepts

The goal of the SCCT is to ensure that every child succeeds, and that school and community members work together to increase the number of students who arrive each day ready to learn.

The SCCT:

* Provides a platform to deliver prevention, early intervention, and more intensive intervention services at or through the school.
* Employs a school-wide referral system to address health, mental health, and social/behavioral concerns that interfere with student achievement.
* Meets weekly, or at least bi-weekly, to discuss students of concern, develops intervention plans, and reviews the progress of previously developed plans.
* Ensures that all members of the team sign an Oath of Confidentiality, a statement of their responsibility to protect confidential information of students and their families discussed before the Care Team.
* Develops assistance plans that are strength-based and combines programs and resources with professional services to form a "network of support".
* Provides oversight and coordination of intervention plans for multiple students at each meeting.

* Keeps records of the discussion, the School Coordinated Services Plans developed for students, and the follow-up progress of the students.
* Develops partnerships with community agencies and programs that are formalized through a Memorandum Of Understanding (MOU) with the school or district.
* Measures program effectiveness jointly with the school district and partnership agencies.
* Assists, based on the knowledge learned from student issues brought before it, in the provision of opportunities, services and supports at both the preventative level (often referred to as Tier I), the early intervention services level (Tier II), as well as more intensive services for students who present severe and chronic problems (Tier III).
* Provides a report to the school and district on any trends the team has recorded on the issues presented to the Care Team by students that require a new or revised program, and/or services at the school site and district level.

Resource Coordination Tips

* Map out and develop a list of community agencies, clinics and other professional practitioners serving your school community.
* Research what resources, both formal and informal, are being utilized by school staff.
* Conduct an assessment of your school community, identifying needs and resources, as well as identified service and program gaps.
* Check to make sure that the agency and its staff are culturally sensitive and inclusive, and are accepting and welcoming of people who represent various lifestyle choices.
* Keep a file that catalogues the resources available, including the name of the agency or provider, the initial contact person, address and phone number, along with any specific requirements or eligibility for the service(s).
* Check to see how community services are linking with the existing student support structures within the school, including the School Coordinated Care Team, the Student Success Team and the School Attendance Review Team.
* Have an initial one-on-one meeting with community agency staff toward building collaborative relationships.
* Host an orientation for all community partners serving your school.
* Hold a resource fair during lunch or after school for both students and caregivers.
* Align services with your school site plan.

- Create a school "information tool kit" for your partners, including school hours of operation, bell schedule, phone numbers, staff list, school rules and procedures, and emergency protocols.
- Develop MOU's outlining the expectations and responsibilities of the school and its partners.
- Provide a space in your school for community partners to utilize.
- Provide resources, such as a telephone and computer, for your community partners to use when they are working in the school.
- Maintain ongoing communication with your community partners regarding the service needs of the students/families.
- Include information about community partners and available resources in newsletters, on bulletin boards, and at meetings for parents and for staff.
- Invite community partners to school events and meetings.
- Provide ongoing recognition of your community partners.
- Conduct collaborative feedback and evaluations of the services provided.

References

1 Ginott, Hiam G., *Between Parent and Child*, New York, Three Rivers Press, 1965, (Revised and updated in 2003 by Dr. Alice Ginott and Dr. Wallace Goddard).

2 Pre-Referral Intervention Manual: The Most Common Learning and Behavior Problems Encountered in the Educational Environment, Columbia, MO, Hawthorne Educational Services, Inc.

3 The Dalai Lama and Cutler, Howard, *The Art of Happiness: A Handbook for Living*, Hodder and Stoughton, 2009, page 69.

The Student Success Team (SST) Philosophy and Implementation

The SST philosophy is based on the belief that the school, home and community need to work together to assist the student with obstacles that become evident in the school setting. The SST is a strength-based process and inquiry that seeks to set a course for assisting the student, build a network of support, coordinate the supportive efforts, implement a variety of interventions, and monitor the results.

The purpose of the meeting is to seek positive solutions for maximizing a student's potential.

The SST meeting is a collaborative process that follows a defined process, progressing through the topics/columns on the SST Summary Form. The discussion always starts with the left-hand column of the SST Summary Form by identifying and acknowledging the strengths of the student. (Examples of the SST Summary Forms can be found in the SST appendix in multiple languages.) The Student Success Team (SST) process helps to support student success by bringing together the following:

* The student: The inclusion of the student is paramount to the buy-in of the plan that will be developed on his/her behalf.
* The parents or guardians: Their experiences and perspectives are important sources of information, and again, paramount to the buy-in of the plan.
* Core members of the Student Success Team such as the facilitator and recorder.
* Other appropriate school staff such as a resource teacher, school counselor, school social worker, or a school nurse.
* Other people who are familiar with the student and who can be supportive. Some of these might include a relative, a community worker, or a therapist.

The SST process creates a structure and forum to bring these partners together for their input, the expression of their concerns, to share their ideas, and to commit to those action items to which they have agreed, thereby being part of the solution.

DOI: 10.4324/9781003240266-3

When the circle of communication is joined between all of the partners, and the student gets the clear message that those significant people in his/her life really want the best for them, both in school and in life, positive changes can and do occur.

Some benefits of the SST process

* Provides a forum for determining appropriate strategies and best practices to meet the needs of individual students.
* Provides a way for students to gain control and have influence over their own learning and school experience.
* Provides documentation of the actions/interventions for the student on behalf of the student.
* Serves as a coordination mechanism for collaboration between school, home and community which emphasizes the positive efforts contributed by each party.
* Economical, efficient, focused meetings with built-in follow-up to provide accountability.
* Analysis of SST data can serve as a tool to support ongoing instructional improvement such as informing grade level and whole school level professional development. It can also help to inform the need for program development and/or program modifications.

Four Themes that are "Key" to the SST Process

1. Build on the strengths of the student and the family

We are all aware that the student would not be in the SST process if s/he were not experiencing some barrier to success in school. Nevertheless, in every student's life something is working, and it is the job of the team to discover and utilize what that is. What is critical to a successful SST process is for the Student Success Team to discover—through observation, investigation and discussion—*how we can build upon those things that are already working in the student's life.*

Research studies, like those of the Search Institute, have shown that the more personal assets/strengths a student has, both internal and external, the more likely they will be to have the resiliency to bounce back from any negativity in their life. Such a listing of assets can be found both through the Search Institute [1] or through the material presented from Project Cornerstone: Developmental Assets and Social/Emotional Learning.[2]

Student improvement in all areas will happen more quickly, more frequently, and more uniformly when a student's strengths are acknowledged and built upon in constructing a plan to address those things that are getting in the way of the student's success.

It is important that the SST team and the SST process address the following questions:

* Where has the student found success in their life?
* Where has the family found success in supporting the student?
* What part of the student's life is unique and successful?
* What is happening in those unique situations and settings that allow for that success?
* What are the passions, interests, "super powers", hobbies, skills, talents and likes that the student has used to find that success?

Much of the power of this approach is that the student has already embraced these unique successes, and these successes are already familiar and culturally understood by the student and her or his family.

These unique successes will be the road map to building a plan for the future success of the student and open the door to understanding the situation through the student's eyes, which will enhance the chances of success.

2. Parent/guardian and student buy-in

Unlike the School Coordinated Care Team, the SST almost always includes the student and his/her caregivers. *A Student Success Team meeting is not considered a true SST unless the parent(s)/guardian(s) and the student are present and participate in the collaborative process. Not having the student and/or caregivers at an SST should always be the exception. People whose lives are affected by the decision need to be part of the decision-making process.*

We do not have the power, nor should we, to mandate what others should do on their own behalf. As much as possible, we must join with the student and their parent(s)/guardian(s) to find solutions to overcome what is getting in the way of a student's success.

> This buy-in of the student and his/her caregivers will help increase the chance of a plan of success. As previously stated, it is very important for the student and the caregiver(s) to see that this process is being done with them, not to them. They are full partners in the decisions that will be made collaboratively on behalf of our shared responsibility, the student.

The SST Team should always be encouraged to invite those individuals who are familiar with the student and can provide input and ideas, and who can undertake parts of the Action Plan. These might include a favorite aunt or uncle, a person to help interpret, a mentor or Court Appointed Special Advocate (CASA), a mental health clinician, an important religious person to the student, or a probation officer. It is not uncommon to have four to seven people in addition to the student, caregiver(s), and the school support staff to participate in the SST meeting process.

3. **Make the problem the problem**

Steve likes to say that "the problem is the problem" and of course he is correct. How often do schools confuse the person with the "problem"? It can be too easy to label the student as a "problem student" or a "lazy student" or an "angry student".

* Identifying a problem(s) that the student may have does not define his/her entire being, and, if we're not careful, has the potential to reinforce the belief that s/he is the problem.
* If we don't separate the student from the problem, it becomes difficult to see them in a new way, and makes it difficult for change to occur.

Language is very powerful. We must also be very careful of terms such as "always" or "never" as we work through an SST meeting process, as those terms rarely apply to any situation or person, and can make it very difficult for change to take place.

"Johnny **never** listens and is **always** out of his seat" can be re-framed as "Johnny has trouble staying on task when he is doing his math", or "Johnny is out of his seat 50% of the time". This allows for a baseline that you can show progress from and gives space for change to come about.

Other examples of separating the student from the problem:

"I like you but I don't like your behavior.
That behavior or way of thinking gets in the way of me enjoying you."
(See A Paradigm Shift: Finding Students' Strengths from Their Stumbling Blocks later in this chapter.)

Nevertheless, as a school, we cannot accept negative behavior that gets in the way of a student learning or a student being successful. There must be consequences for these behaviors. Our goal should be to eliminate the negative behaviors, or ways of thinking, but very rarely should the goal be to eliminate the student. That should take place only when another setting may be more appropriate for the student's success.

Our work and efforts should always be about the student going in the right direction.....and should not be about the student reaching perfection.
We should always remember to celebrate a student heading in a better direction.

4. **The need for follow-up: Built-in Accountability**

No matter how good a plan for success might be, it is only as good as the follow-up that occurs. The pieces of the plan literally need to be "glued together" or, unfortunately, the entire effort will be wasted. The first meeting solidifies the partnership and defines the "road map". What happens from that point forward is what will determine the success of the plan. In following up, we need to make sure the plan we developed is doing what we want it to do.

An essential component of the SST process is ensuring that each SST meeting have at least one, or possibly more, follow-up meetings. The follow-up meetings serve a number of functions that assist in maintaining accountability in the process. They include:

* Evaluating the effect of previously agreed upon interventions and adding new information that has come to light.
* Setting a new course, or modifying previous actions/interventions that have not been successful.
* Making appropriate referrals for assessment for Section 504 accommodations, Special Education eligibility, or other specialized programs and services.
* Celebrating successes and providing closure on the matter, if indicated.

Cultural Awareness and Understanding Within the SST Process

1. As educators who are working with an at-risk population, we must be very sensitive and aware of the cultural differences with the students and families we are working with.
2. We must always remember that the way we see the world is just the way we see the world, and might not be the way the student and family see the world. With this in mind, the "building on a student's and family's strengths" takes on a more powerful meaning.
3. Many times, as we assess a student's school and home situation, we come to a better understanding of what changes need to take place for the student to become more successful. These strategies/interventions/actions must be done within the context of their culture, and the belief system of those who care for them.
4. Because of our training and experience, many times these understandings and conclusions are very valid and will indeed help support the student's success. The downside of these understandings and conclusions can be an unintentional ignoring of the cultural trappings of the student and family.
5. What will take on a deeper level of understanding will be the SST focusing on what is already working in the life of the student and family. What is already working, by its very nature, has been accepted as culturally sensitive and acceptable by both the student and his/her family. Thus, we must be diligent in fostering and building upon the elements of success that are already working within the life of the student and their family.

Getting Started

Student Success Team Roles

Individuals need to be selected who can fill these roles in order for the Student Success Team to function. These defined roles are meant to be fluid, meaning that a particular role can be shifted from one to another. This "shifting" of roles can happen at various points in the year, or when a specific member of the team would be the best to facilitate.

What cannot be emphasized enough is the crucial role of the person who coordinates the pre-meeting SST responsibilities. There is no getting around the fact that pulling the meeting(s) together takes time, and can easily be a key component of a student support professional's job description. Similar to the roles defined in the Care Team, it is possible that a school counselor, school social worker, a dean, or an administrator may choose to take on this role.

It is not uncommon for people to show up for an SST meeting only to find out that the teacher had not been given sufficient notice of the time and place for the meeting, arrangements had not been made for the parent(s)/guardian(s) to be able to attend, the necessary equipment was not in the room, or nobody had spoken with the student about the purpose of the SST meeting, and how they could contribute to the process.

If the arrangements and necessary outreach does not happen so that an SST goes smoothly, it certainly will not.

Coordinator of all pre-SST meetings

* Coordinates all logistics before the meeting.
* Notifies those key individuals of the time, place and student(s) scheduled, and what they are expected to bring to the meeting.
* Must have good communication skills and an inviting tone, because this person might be the first to communicate with the student's home. They should be able to answer any questions the family might have about the SST meeting and process. The pre-meeting facilitator ensures that the caregiver(s) receive an SST preparation brochure/packet. The SST brochure is a good overview for families, but cannot take the place of personal contact, encouragement, and assistance when needed to help them attend the meeting (e.g., transportation, child watch/care, translator/interpreter). See sample of an SST brochure in the SST Appendix.
* Ensures that the student receives an explanation of the SST process and a brochure that contains questions for them to answer about school, their strengths, skills and hobbies. Coming into a room with a number of adults unprepared can be very uncomfortable.
* Ensures that the "trace and tracking" information regarding the student be available for the meeting (e.g., "cum" folder, scholarship record, test scores, attendance record, current teacher input form(s), grades in progress, or work samples).
* Ensures that those who will be presenting information at the meeting have the necessary materials and documentation ready.

- Ensures that each member of the team for a particular student, both the core members and student specific individuals, are informed of the time, place and date of the scheduled SST meeting.
- Ensures that the meeting room is properly prepared (e.g., SST banner and header are in place, electronic or other recording device are available and working, recording tools are present, and chairs are arranged in either a semi-circle, or other inclusive setup).

(Due to the commitment of time and effort it will take for the pre-meeting Coordinator to pull together and prepare for each SST meeting, if this responsibility is not a key component of the individual's job description, it would be a good idea to compensate this person in some way. Either by a stipend or by some other means to show appreciation for their over and above effort).

Facilitator during the SST meeting

- Knows that the primary role is to facilitate, not to present information.
- Usually stands in front of the group, often configured as a semi-circle.
- Needs to make sure that the purpose of the meeting is clear: The success of the student.
- Is supportive, knowledgeable and empowered to lead.
- Helps the recorder to take accurate notes.
- Checks for meaning/understanding.
- Encourages comments from all team members by asking "any questions", "any additions"?
- Keeps group focused on the purpose of the meeting.
- Asks for specifics, not generalities.
- Is positive, and ensures a positive feeling tone.
- Is non-judgmental, and encourages others to do the same.
- Defuses emotionally charged statements.
- Sees that the team prioritizes concerns and actions.
- Helps the team to find win/win solutions for teachers, students, and caregivers.

The recorder

- Ensures that the SST Summary Form, or SST Follow-Up Form, accurately represents and records the input, ideas and decisions made during the meeting.
- Keeps a record of all meetings and a copy of the SST Summary/Action Plans, and follow-up meetings for each student.
- Writes legibly.
- Keeps information organized.
- Shortens, abbreviates.

Team members

* Contribute information and their perspective to the discussion, and help to define the action items that will be undertaken.
* Function as a team more than as individuals.
* Have knowledge of resources, and how to access them.
* Avoid side conversations.
* Assume responsibility for actions, when appropriate.

The time keeper:

* Helps the facilitator to keep the meeting going forward so that all of the items for discussion can be addressed. The time keeper may signal the facilitator that it is time to move on.

SST Facilitator: Observation Checklist

It is important that facilitators, particularly those who are new or less experienced, are able to practice the facilitation process in front of their peers, in order to strengthen their skills. We like to call it an "art", and it does take practice to do an effective job. Most of us were not trained in this skill in our professional preparation programs, no matter what the discipline was. Like other aspects of the SST process, the critique provided is meant to be a positive, and offered in a way that the person who tries out the facilitation process sees as a useful tool for improvement.

For all SST meetings make sure that:

* The purpose and process of the SST meeting are clearly stated at the beginning.
* The student's strengths are the first item discussed.
* The input from the caregiver(s) and the student are sought in the first ten minutes.
* The areas of concern are prioritized and discussed.
* Every column/topic on the SST Summary is discussed.
* A "broad range of interventions" are considered (classroom, larger school, in/with the home, in/with the community).
* The caregiver(s) and student input are solicited in Action Planning.
* The student strengths are considered when selecting Interventions.
* The responsibility for each action item is assigned.
* A completion date is assigned for each item.
* The facilitator reads the Action items to ensure consensus.
* A follow-up date is set.
* All team members sign and receive a copy of the Action Plan.

For Follow-up meetings make sure that:

* The SST facilitator checks in with each team member regarding implementation of previously agreed upon Action items.
* The progress toward each desired student outcome is considered.
* New information is discussed.
* New concerns are discussed, if appropriate.
* A new Action Plan is developed, if appropriate.

What Happens at the SST Meeting?

* The student and his/her parent(s)/guardian(s) meet with the others who have gathered together for the SST meeting. The "core" members of the SST include the facilitator, recorder, timekeeper, and other possible regular members of the team. Others, such as school staff who have a specific connection to the particular student (e.g., teacher(s) or counselors of the student) would also be invited to the meeting. In addition to school staff, the family is encouraged to bring those individuals whom they would like to be part of the process (e.g., a step-parent, favorite aunt or uncle, therapist, or probation officer). It is not uncommon to have six to ten people in addition to the student and his/her caregiver(s) to be involved in the meeting.
* Once everyone has arrived, the facilitator thanks them for coming and asks each person to introduce themselves and their relationship to the student. The facilitator states the purpose of the meeting and then starts to guide the group through a process that results in a written Action Plan.
* The recorder captures the discussion either by writing on a large "banner" under each of the columns, on an overhead projector with the columns defined, or on a computerized version of the topics to be discussed. It is extremely useful if everyone can see what is being written as the meeting progresses in order for them to follow the process toward the development of the SST Summary or Action Plan.
* The meeting always starts with a discussion of the strengths of the student, asking each person at the meeting to share a strength, or something positive about the student. The next column is where information is gathered, and listed in the Known Information column (e.g., current grades and credits, test results, relevant medical information, or family composition). The agenda proceeds with a discussion of the interventions/modifications that have already been attempted to address the issues of concern, and what the results have been.
* The process continues with a listing of the concerns of the school, the student, the parent(s)/guardian(s) and/or others. These are listed in the Concerns/Things Getting in the Way column. After the list has been generated, the group can prioritize the items enumerated.

* The next column is Questions, and this is the place to list those things that the team would like to know more about. It might require speaking with someone not at the meeting, or gathering additional information.
* Following a discussion of the concerns, everyone is asked to "brainstorm" ideas based on what they have heard thus far with regard to the strengths of the student, what has already been tried and the results, and the concerns that have been expressed. The "brainstormed" ideas should be listed with respect to everyone's input, and the team can then prioritize those ideas that will most likely become part of the SST Summary Form.
* The Actions column is where the actual plan will be recorded, and where the actions or interventions can be prioritized.
* It is important that not too much of the responsibility be put on the student, the parent(s)/guardian(s), or any other members of the team. As much as possible, each person should have some responsibility for implementation of a specific action item.
* The next column is the "who" and then the "when" this action is expected to be implemented. (It is suggested that the team does not use terms such "as soon as possible" to the when, and to be as specific as possible).
* The team decides on a follow-up date which is then recorded, everyone present is asked to sign the document to record their participation. The recorder will then make copies of the plan which was developed, and provide a copy for each member who has gathered.

Teacher (T)/Counselor(C) Preparation Checklist for an SST Meeting: (Also appropriate for the School Coordinated Care Team (SCCT) and the School Attendance Review Team SART)

Review the student's "cum" (cumulative) folder and other records, paying particular attention to:

* History of standardized achievement test data (T).
* Current and past attendance and tardy information (C).
* Academic record and current grades in progress (T).
* Hearing and vision screening results, health issues (C).
* School history, including retention(s), referrals to various programs/services (C).
* History of contacts with the family (C/T).

Be prepared to present specific background information about the student:

* Strengths to build upon (C/T).
* Interests, hobbies, skills (C/T).
* Academic performance in reading, oral language, written language (T).
* Amount and quality of class work and homework (T).

Be ready to discuss:

* Strategies and modifications that have been tried and what the results have been (T/C).
* Efforts to work with the family to address your concerns (T/C).
* Your concern or concerns (academic, behavioral, social-emotional, or health) (T/C).
* Desired student outcomes (the improvements you would like to see as outcomes) (T/C).

Bring to the SST meeting:

* Student's cumulative file (C).
* Recent work samples that reflect strengths and areas of concern (T).
* In-class assessments that show academic levels (T).

Including Parents/Guardians as Team Members

Parents and students are full-fledged members of the SST, and, as previously stated, they are *always* included. In fact, if the parent and student are not present, it is not considered an SST meeting. The parent/guardian can share the familial perspective and concerns, contribute critical information from the home, and share effective and ineffective home interventions. Many times, the parent can clarify questions for the team and participate in the implementation of strategies/actions developed by the whole team.

A Note on Outreach to Parents/Guardians

Engaging the parent(s)/guardian(s) is a key element in making the SST process successful. This effort involves much more than sending a written notice of a meeting or making a simple phone call. It involves extending oneself as a representative of the school and serving as a "bridge" for the parent/guardian to enter the school environment.

Sometimes parents/guardians resist this attempt to engage them. The barriers to their involvement might mask deeper fears and concerns. Being the parent/guardian of a student with school and/or social concerns can cause the parent to have feelings of defensiveness or guilt. Many parents feel they, or their child, will be unfairly attacked or made to feel worse than they already do in an SST meeting. They might have had previous experiences with school meetings that were not successful, or they were not kept well informed, and they might be reluctant to trust another meeting at the school, or representatives of the school or school system.

The person performing the outreach/engagement role must be sensitive to these issues. Information about the purpose of the meeting must be presented with an emphasis on the shared concerns and responsibilities. An explanation of the SST system must be provided, emphasizing that the process is a collaborative one that builds upon the student's strengths in order to attain the highest degree of success for the student. The caregivers must also be given an opportunity to ask any questions or share with the upcoming meeting any concerns they might have.

Caregivers might also have time, work, childcare or transportation issues complicating their participation in the meeting. The SST process must include support to parents to accommodate these very real issues. Any support provided has both symbolic and concrete meaning to the caregivers, and contributes to the success of the meeting for both parents and team members.

A Brief Note About the Absent Parent, Most Often the Father

Many schools accept a statement from the custodial parent that the absent parent is "out of the picture", and the school should/will only deal with them, the custodial parent. This could be a huge mistake because the absence of one of the parents may be one of the main underlying reasons for the student's alienation from school, depression, acting out or dropping out. If the absent parent is anywhere in the geographical area, it is a worthwhile effort to reach out to this parent, and let them know how important it is to the school that they become involved in their child's education, and by extension, their life as well. Even if there is "bad blood" between the biological parents, they should know that their offspring needs the involvement of both parents if their youngster is to be successful, as well as the negative implications if they continue not to be involved. To the extent that the absent parent gets re-involved with their offspring, this can serve as part of the "solution" to the presenting problems, and for the student to become more successful.

What Do Parents Really want from the School and its Personnel?

First and foremost, the caregiver(s) want to know that you, or your team, as representatives of the school, have the best interest of their child at heart, and that you truly want to join with them for the benefit of their youngster. If the caregivers believe that their child is really cared about, we believe this can transcend any racial, ethnic or language barriers. They also want to know that you, and the other members of the team, are people of integrity. They will not be able to determine that until after you have worked together, and they see that you, and the other members of the team, are people who follow through on the commitments they have made, and do not disappoint them. When this is achieved, the caregivers are much more willing to trust in, and join with, the team, in the interest of their child/student.

Including Students as Team Members

The student is an essential part of the SST meeting. As will be said a number of times in this book, *"We can't do this to them, only with them."* Involving the student in decisions that affect his or her life is empowering for the student, and models the kind of collaborative relationship that has the best chance for success. If the student does not assume some responsibility for actions that could benefit them, it will be very difficult for the process to be successful.

When the student enters the room and sees the number of important adults in his or her life who have gathered together on their behalf, a powerful message of caring and commitment to their success is given. Considering that the adults have busy schedules and they have all found a way to come together on their behalf, the importance of the occasion, and the potential importance to the student's future, is evident. The student clearly gets this powerful message, even if she or he is not overjoyed at the reason to attend the meeting at the onset.

Orientation to the meeting is important for the student. It is useful to have some member of the team to meet with the student prior to the SST meeting to answer questions about the purpose and process of the SST. During this orientation meeting students can be asked to complete a brief, open-ended questionnaire about their likes and dislikes regarding school, future goals, and what they would like to see come out of the meeting. It is useful for the caregivers to complete a similar questionnaire that will help to give the team insight into their perspective. When the purpose of the meeting is explained to the student and caregiver(s), and they hear that they are equal members of the team, and their input is welcomed and necessary, most respond positively.

(Please see a sample brochure in both English and Spanish that appear in the Appendix).

Students can share their strengths, their areas of concern, and can participate in the determination of success strategies, as well as their role and responsibility for implementing them. The student receives support and assistance from the adults on the team who take responsibility for actions on the students' behalf with the goal of positive change. The powerful effect that the listing of his or her strengths by these significant adults has for a student's self-image cannot be underestimated.

A Note on Involving Younger Children in the SST Process

It is perfectly appropriate to include very young children in the SST process. Even young children know when their parents/guardians are coming to school, and they may wonder or become anxious about what is going on in the meeting. An easy way to demystify the meeting is to invite the young child into the meeting. Even the youngest child is able to share what he or she likes and dislikes about school, and might be able to express ideas about what would make school more successful for them.

At the discretion of the facilitator and/or caregiver, younger children might be asked to step outside or go back to their classroom while the caregiver shares sensitive information that they would prefer the child not to hear. However, the fact that sensitive information will be shared at some point in the meeting should not be used as a reason to exclude the student from the meeting. Another option for handling sensitive information would be to list as an action item a follow-up meeting between the caregiver and a member of the Student Success Team.

In any case, every child should be present for the recitation of the student's strengths because of its obvious positive effect on the student. Helping the child to feel comfortable in the meeting is the first step to their feeling comfortable working with the adults on a school success plan.

SST Header and Banner to Develop the Group Memory

(Please see samples of the SST Summary Form, and the SST follow-up form in the SST Appendix)

The "Header and Banner"

In the original SST manual, the "header" referred to is a 6½ feet by one foot plastic-coated chart containing the pre-printed elements/columns of the SST process. Typically, this "header" is placed on the wall facing all of the members gathered for the SST meeting. Blank butcher paper is then placed below the header and affixed to the "header" via the use of tape. The butcher paper is what is referred to as the "banner". The recorder of the meeting lists the comments made by team members on the banner, lining them up underneath the appropriate columns/titles on the "header". These comments constitute the group memory.

* The combination of the header and the banner underneath is used as a focus to structure the communication process during the SST meeting. By recording the "group memory" in front of those who have gathered, it allows everyone to see not only what is being recorded, but to get a clearer "picture" of the student. Even a person who does not know the student at the start of the meeting will see a "picture" of the student start to emerge as the banner is completed.
* The "banner" provides a place to document the team's positive intervention plan. The information from the banner is copied at the end of the meeting, and duplicated for all parties, especially those who will have some responsibility for part of the SST Summary Form that was developed at the meeting.

We understand that times have changed and it may seem "old-fashioned" to follow a paper procedure such as the one described. With modern technology, some schools are using a computerized version of the "header/banner" that is connected to a computer that projects the SST Summary Form onto a wall. Participants can follow as items are being typed on the computer as the process unfolds. At times, the SST might utilize an overhead projector or a "white board" to do the same thing, although these are somewhat more cumbersome.

> The SST header is a "road map", a sequential agenda that, if followed, provides both a natural and positive flow to the SST meeting, and a complete record of the discussion. We believe it is crucial for all members of the team to be able to see the process unfold right in front of them. This visual process also serves to keep the discussion focused on the columns/topics being discussed, and helps the facilitator and recorder to keep the discussion within the time frame allotted for the meeting, typically 45–60 minutes.

Since the SST process is a positive, strength-based inquiry, the "strengths" section always comes first. Proceeding through relevant topics/columns on the header often has the effect of illuminating the nature and complexity of a concerns about the student that affect his or her school experience. No section/column should be ignored or given too much emphasis.

(Please see examples of a completed SST Summary Form that is considered exemplary, and one that was completed in a seriously limited way in the SST Appendix.) Additionally, if the paper form of the SST Summary is utilized, it would be a good idea to expand the form to 8½" by 14" to allow people more space for input.)

A. The Strengths Column

After an introduction to the purpose of the meeting, the facilitator will ask each person gathered to state something they see that is positive, or a strength of the student, including asking the student him/herself the same question. It is very important for the student to hear that other important people to the student recognize positive things about them such as their interests, their hobbies, their passions, and other things they do well. This has a symbolic meaning even though before long the team will be talking about this student's challenges, or the things that are getting in the way of success. As Steve likes to say, "everyone has something that is working for them, and our recognition of this fact starts the meeting off on a positive note".

B. Known Information/Modifications Column

All pertinent information regarding the student should be listed in the Known Information column. Basic vision and hearing results, and other relevant medical information, should be listed here. Academic levels, school history (particularly if the student has been in a number of schools), attendance, family composition, and significant events happening in the home that are relevant to the student's situation, can also be listed here. Previous efforts to assist the student, such as modifications and interventions that have been tried, and how they have worked, are listed in this column that is often split into two sections for that reason. The team can rate the effectiveness of these efforts with a "+" for those that have been effective, and "−" for those that have had little or no effect.

During this discussion the team might ask questions of the caregivers such as:

* Who does the student live with?
* Has there been any significant childhood illness or conditions?
* When was the last time the student had a physical?
* What language is spoken in the home?
* How does this student spend his/her time after school?
* Any significant events or changes in the student's life (e.g., moves or losses)?

C. Concerns/What's Getting in the Way Column

(Please note that the SST Summary Form shown in the Appendix does not say, "What's getting in the way" next to Concerns, but the authors believe that all future SST Summary Forms should include this as well. The emphasis here is not only to express the "concerns" of the various parties, but to re-frame them as things that are getting in the way of the student's success).

As mentioned earlier, schools must remember that "the problem is the problem", not the student or his/her family. The team lists the "concerns/the things getting in the way", that the school thinks are keeping the student from being more successful. The team then proceeds to prioritize the concerns/the things getting in the way, in this column, such as academic, social/emotional, physical, attendance, or behavioral issues. Caution should be taken not to label the student but to list the observable behavior(s). The team should limit concerns to the most pressing ones, usually three or four. The team should then prioritize numerically which concern the team will address first, second, and so forth.

(*Note:* If the same concerns occur frequently for many students who have an SST, or if the team sees other patterns/trends during this portion of SST discussions, as has already been said, this would represent the need for a "systemic" response).

D. The Questions Column

This column allows the entire team to voice questions related to the discussion. This is a time to clarify issues and to note those questions or issues that may need to be revisited.

E. The Strategies Column (Brainstorming)

One of the most critical elements in the SST process is "brainstorming". At this point in the meeting, the entire team looks back at the student's strengths and the concerns/those things that are getting in the way, and "brainstorms" strategies to address these. The whole idea of brainstorming is to relax the censor inside the mind so that creative thinking can run free. This is the place to think outside of the box. Have fun with this phase of the process! The more ideas you develop, the better. The strategies/interventions are typically grouped into four areas for intervention, previously referred to as the "broad range of interventions". In the next phase of the meeting, the team will have an opportunity to convert the brainstormed ideas into action items.

F. The Actions Column

Use the Brainstorming List for Action Planning:

* Look over the list.
* Select the ideas that emerge from the list that seem workable.
* Combine ideas if you wish.
* Prioritize and select actions.

This column is the place for developing an "Action Plan" (sometimes referred to as a Service Plan or an Intervention Plan), which is really the prescriptive plan for improvement. It details the responsibilities to be assumed by the teacher, the parent(s)/guardian(s), the student, school support staff, and community resource persons. The Action Plan should be reasonable and reflect a positive, doable, and supportive effort to restore the student to a successful school experience.

For example, "to do homework" is a goal, but not an action item. An action item is what the SST recommends to support and assist a student in doing his or her homework, such as to use a school homework center, turn off the TV, or create a separate area at home for doing homework.

The team prioritizes the list of strategies/interventions and selects those actions that have the most potential for success, based on the student's strengths, and that address the concern(s)/the things getting in the way. The actions should be shared equally by the student, family, school, and, when appropriate, community resources and/or programs. In no circumstance should the actions listed here be phrased to suggest blame or to place the sole responsibility for action(s) on the student or the parent/guardian.

G. Who Column

A specific person is listed as a responsible party for implementing an action. Individuals not in attendance at the SST meeting should not be given responsibility for an action.

However, a team member at the meeting may list as an action item that he or she will request the assistance of a person who is not at the meeting.

H. When Column

A specific date of initiation of any new action is listed in this column. In most instances this is done by suggesting an actual date. If determining an exact date is not possible because a referral to a service needs to be completed first, and if that service date is not available at the time of the meeting, the date may be listed by "future date". Indeterminate dates should be avoided, such as "ASAP", "immediately", or "ongoing". As has been said in a number of places, follow-up is very important on the actions developed at Student Success Team (SST) meetings, as are those decided in the School Coordinated Care Team (SCCT) meetings, and/or in the School Attendance Review Team (SART) conferences.

The SST Process and its Relationship to the Assessment for Special Education or Section 504 of the Federal Rehabilitation Code of 1973

The Student Success Team is a process that works to benefit students with the programs, resources, services and supports available to ALL students within the regular education environment.

> The fact that the SST process is a function of regular education is very important to remember.

There are some who think that you only refer a student for an SST when they need to be formally assessed for Special Education services. In fact, the SST can and should be utilized for any student who is not being successful. An SST can be held when it is felt that addressing what is getting in the way of student success will be best served by bringing together the student, the parent(s)/guardian(s), school staff, and an involved community representative, for problem solving and direction setting.

Most of the students who move through the SST process will not be referred for consideration of Special Education services or Section 504 accommodations. However, when and if the Student Success Team feels that is has done its due diligence in working to maximize a student's potential within the regular education environment, and there is a consensus that the student may have a qualifying condition for Special Education services or Section 504 accommodations, those will be listed as Action items on the SST plan, along with when this will occur and who is responsible.

> To that extent, the SST is most always the entry point to an assessment to determine eligibility for Special Education services or Section 504 accommodations, and that is also very important to remember.

Both Special Education services and Section 504 of the Rehabilitation Code of 1973 are based on Federal law. If the student is referred for a formal assessment or consideration for either of these services, the SST will be asked to provide documentation of a conscientious effort to help the student address his/her barriers to greater success within the regular education environment, as well as any other documentation required by the district to support this/these referral(s).

Therefore, *the SST has dual functions:*

* The first is to bring services and supports within the regular education environment.
* The second is to help decide which students should be referred for Special Education assessment or Section 504 accommodations.

The SST process is a very powerful and important function, which should be in place at every school.

Because of the limited resources available at the school, utilizing the filtering/funneling process described in this manual is the best way to intervene effectively on behalf of a student in an organized way, while helping to ensure that the student receives any and all of the services to which they are entitled or eligible.

The fact is that the SST process is neither a direct line to Special Education or Section 504 accommodations, nor should it serve as a roadblock to an assessment for such services.

SST Best Practices Checklist

Pre-SST meeting

* It is important to designate core members of the team in addition to the occasional members who will be different for each student.
* There is a designated person who coordinates the SST process.
* There is a referral process in place that uses a Request for Service Form, along with other documentation if the student was discussed in Intervention areas I, II, and III. (An example of this form is provided in the SST Appendix).
* School staff are aware of the SST process, and who the coordinator is.
* Core members of the Student Success Team need to be identified. These people will most often attend all SST meetings. The roles they assume (e.g., facilitator, recorder, or timekeeper) are fluid and interchangeable at various points in time, such as at the end of a semester. Others attending the SST are "student specific", those who have knowledge of, or a relationship to the student.
* The parent/guardian receives a meeting notice along with the SST Parent Brochure in their home language, and in a timely manner.

- A member of the team assumes responsibility to "outreach" to the caregiver(s) to discuss the purpose of the meeting, and to address any barriers to their attendance. While the brochure is a good overview for families, it cannot take the place of personal contact, encouragement, and assistance when needed. This is often an important first step in developing a working relationship with the caregiver(s).
- If the referring teacher will be attending the SST meeting, the teacher receives a Teacher Preparation Checklist prior to the SST meeting, or a Teacher Input Form if the referring teacher will be unable to attend.
- The student is prepared for what to expect at the SST meeting, and given an opportunity to clarify any questions they might have.
- The SST coordinator should make the necessary arrangements, including that a room is available, all participants are notified as to time and place, and roles are defined in advance.
- The coordinator ensures that relevant material is available at the meeting (e.g., cum folder, scholarship record, test scores, or attendance record) and the SST Summary Chart posted on the wall, or set up on the computer that can project the process for all in attendance to see.

During the SST meeting

- Core team members are consistent in attending the meeting.
- An interpreter/translator is provided when the language of the home is not English.
- The facilitator welcomes the caregiver, allows for introductions of those gathered, and explains the purpose and process of the SST meeting. Special attention should be given to addressing the student, explaining that this meeting is for and about them, but not something being done to them, but rather with them, and their input is most welcome. (This core belief and best practice is repeated a number of times in this book because of how important it is to the collaborative process).
- It is very important, at the meeting, to have everyone introduced, and for them to state their relationship to the student. Next, the facilitator draws attention to the wall chart (or technological alternative) with an explanation of how the process will unfold.
- Starting on the left side of the "header" (wall chart) student strengths are listed. A discussion of the strengths of the student should always be the first discussion item. This sets a positive tone for the meeting, and gives everyone an opportunity to be heard, thus setting the stage for equal input and respectful listening. If there are individuals who try to jump ahead with "concerns or problems" before other columns are discussed, they should be reminded of the meeting process.
- All members are encouraged to participate with their respective knowledge, insights and ideas.

- The "broad range of interventions" should be considered in "brainstorming" ideas, some of which will be become part of the Action Plan. Individual actions should be assigned to as many participants as possible, and a timeline defined.
- Make sure that all participants sign the bottom of the Summary Form to verify their attendance, their agreement with the Action Plan, and to the interventions/actions that have been assigned to them.
- Determine a "point person", sometimes referred to as a "case manager" (Please see Chapter 9 on Case (care) Management) as the one who will work to ensure that, between the first meeting and follow-up meeting(s), the plan gets "glued" together.

  If the action items are not implemented, the plan will most likely fail.

- A follow-up meeting is scheduled at the conclusion of the first meeting.
- Completed SST Summary Forms are copied and distributed to the participants of the meeting, a copy for the cumulative folder, and a copy for the student's confidential file, if one exists.
- Meetings start and end on time, 45–60 minutes for an initial SST, and 15–45 minutes for a follow-up SST meeting.

Post-SST meeting

- A record of the meeting is entered into the SST log form that will be kept by the SST recorder. Typically, these are due each semester to the District Office of Student Services.
- Action items are monitored and follow-through on these items occur. Follow-through is crucial if any real change is to occur.
- Members of the original SST are reminded of the date, time and place of scheduled follow-up meetings.

The SST process: Some key components

- The student and their parents/guardians need to be part of the process.
- People whose lives are affected by a decision must, as much as possible, be part of the decision-making process.
- We cannot hope to bring about success for the student by doing it for them, only with them.
- The buy-in of the student and family will be a key factor in bringing about the possibility of improved success.
- All parties to the plan that is developed must feel responsible to own their part of the plan.
- Build on the student's strengths.
- Make the problem the problem, not the student or his/her family.
- Follow-up on meetings is crucial.

Looking at Behaviors through a New Lens

As we attempt to look at behaviors through a new lens, it is very important to understand that stumbling blocks are not acceptable if they get in the way of instruction and learning, and they cannot be tolerated at school or in the classroom. What the reframing allows us to do is to find an opening or a strength to build upon.

A student shouting out an answer rather than raising their hand, can be very disruptive in a classroom setting. But the reframing of the situation can provide an opening to help the student change their behavior. (i.e., "Johnny—quit shouting out the answers or I'll I send you out of the room" can become "Johnny, I love that you know the answer and I love your enthusiasm but I need you to raise your hand before you give me your brilliant answer").

A Paradigm Shift: Finding Students' Strengths from Their Stumbling Blocks

Stumbling Blocks	Strengths
Is conceited; cocky	Has confidence
Is inflexible, closed-minded, rigid	Is consistent, shows discipline
Compromises, lacks initiative	Is cooperative
Demonstrates recklessness	Has courage
Is willful	Demonstrates decisiveness
Has a one-track mind	Shows diligence
Is a perfectionist	Shows care and attention to detail
Shouts out/talks out of turn	Is assertive, demonstrates enthusiasm
Work is too wordy	Shows expressiveness
Is indecisive, lacks commitment	Indicates fair-mindedness, can see both sides
Is wishy-washy	Is flexible
Shows weakness, is weak willed	Shows forgiveness
Is tactless, insensitive, undiplomatic	Demonstrates frankness, honesty
Is stingy, penny-pinching, cheap	Shows frugality
Is extravagant, squanders	Is generous
Is outspoken, blunt	Demonstrates honesty
Lacks self-confidence, is timid	Demonstrates humility
Is obsessive/compulsive, a perfectionist	Shows organization, neatness
Is stubborn, headstrong	Demonstrates persistence
Is manipulative, uses high pressure	Demonstrates persuasiveness
Seems thin-skinned, oversensitive	Shows sensitivity
Is fraudulent or underhanded	Is resourceful

SST Frequently Asked Questions

1 When can we find time to schedule SST meetings?

Trying to find a convenient time for both school staff and caregivers to meet can be a real challenge. Many schools schedule SST meetings either before or after school. If the meetings are held before school, it is important to allow enough time so that the meeting is not too rushed. At the elementary school level, there might be a time in the day when administrators and support staff are available (i.e., after recess or after lunch) and when classroom coverage is available to the teacher by a colleague (i.e., a kindergarten teacher who teaches in the morning may be available in the afternoon). At the secondary level, many schools are moving toward a common "prep", or planning time, for grade level academic teachers to meet. This might be an excellent time to convene an SST meeting if the caregiver(s) are available to meet their student's teachers in the SST format. Some schools have late start times each week to hold special meetings. If it is not possible to find a time for the caregiver to meet with their student's teachers, the grade counselor can represent the input of the teachers, especially if each teacher has completed the Teacher Input form. (A sample of this form is provided in the Appendix). At the high school level, if the student was referred for an SST meeting by a particular teacher, it is helpful for that teacher to be relieved from their classroom duties if the meeting is being held during one of their class periods. In this case, in respect to the teacher's time, s/he should be given the opportunity to present their views of the student's strengths, what they have done to be helpful, how it has worked, what their concerns are, and any suggestions they have to improve the situation. The recorder will list the teacher's input in the appropriate columns.

In any case, FLEXIBILITY is the key. Those who believe in and support the process are usually able to work out some accommodation that meets the scheduling needs of the majority of the team members. Needless to say, the team member who sets up and schedules the SST meetings has to be a bit of a juggler. Prioritizing time for SST meetings can, in the long run, reduce the time in addressing student issues later.

2 Who are the key personnel involved in the SST process?

As has been said, there are both standing members and student specific members for an SST meeting. The so called "standing members" are the facilitator of the meeting process, a recorder who will record the discussion as it moves along, and a general education liaison, especially at the elementary school level. Having a respected general education teacher liaison is particularly important when discussing classroom interventions/modifications, as the other teachers are apt to accept the suggestions of someone whom they see as a peer, rather than "support staff personnel", who often serve as facilitators or recorders of the SST, but who might not have classroom responsibilities. It is also very helpful to have an administrative representative serving as a "core" member of the team. Student specific members of the team are the teacher(s) of the student, the student, the caregiver(s) of the student, other school and/or district level support staff, and community agency personnel who might be involved with the student/family, and other significant individuals, such as advocates and relatives.

The functions of the "core" members of the team are fluid, and roles can be changed from time to time. Additionally, there can be more than one Student Success Team at the school, such as one team for each grade level, or one for each of the "small learning communities".

3 When should a student be considered for an SST meeting?

As recommended in this publication, schools are encouraged to use a "filtering process" that includes interventions/modifications/accommodations at various levels prior to scheduling an SST meeting. Examples might include discussions regarding the student at teacher grade level meetings, the grade level counselor and/or school social worker first attempting to address these issues, or at the school site Care Team. An SST is often recommended when other assistance has not been successful. A student can also be considered for an SST when it is deemed useful to bring the significant people in the life of the student together for discussion and planning. Students can also be referred directly by their parent/guardian, or by a classroom teacher through the on-site SST facilitator.

In some districts the Student Success Team is utilized as a step prior to referral for a formal assessment and consideration of Special Education services or Section 504 accommodations. In the past, many have perceived the SST process as a vehicle for expediting students into Special Education. In reality, the SST is intended to assist students in becoming more successful within the regular education environment in order to avoid a Special Education referral whenever possible. The SST works with all partners in an attempt to bring this about. The SST should neither be a process to expedite a student to a formal assessment for consideration of Special Education or 504 services, or to serve as a roadblock for such a referral.

4 Why should I refer a student for discussion before the Care Team or an SST meeting?

The purpose of both the Care Team and the SST process is to bring together a group of people who all possess different talents, knowledge and expertise toward the goal of helping the student to become as successful as possible, both academically and socially.

The goal is to provide new strategies that address the concerns and tap into the student's strengths. It is hoped that each member who sits on one of these teams will contribute their ideas and accept responsibility for providing some part of the plan that is developed. It is also hoped that the referring person(s) will gain some assistance in addressing their concerns about the student.

5 When are students and parents not appropriate at an SST meeting?

Both students and their caregivers are core members of the SST process. In fact, the SST meeting is not considered a true SST unless these important people are in attendance. Even very young children can participate in at least part of the meeting. It can help the youngster to demystify what is going on in the meeting room as they are aware that their parent(s)/guardian(s) are in the meeting. Almost all students, regardless of their age, can tell the team what they like about school, what they don't like about school, and what things that might make school better for them.

6 Don't students feel overwhelmed when they enter the meeting room and see so many important adults in their life gathered for the SST meeting?

There are two ways to look at this question. Some might feel somewhat overwhelmed and defensive when they first enter the room, knowing that the focus of the meeting is about them, and their progress, or lack of same, in school. On the other hand, when the student sees that a number of important people in his/her life have gathered together on their behalf, a powerful message of caring and commitment to their success is given. Considering that adults all have busy schedules and have found a way to come together on their behalf, the importance of the occasion for their future is evident. The student clearly gets this powerful message, even if he or she is not overjoyed at the reason for this meeting at the beginning. Orientation to the meeting is important for the student and the caregiver(s) as well. It is useful to have a member of the team meet with the student prior to the SST meeting to answer questions about the process and purpose of the SST meeting. During this orientation meeting the student might be asked to complete a brief, open-ended questionnaire about their likes and dislikes regarding school, future goals, and what they would like to see come out of the meeting. When the purpose of the meeting is explained to students, and they hear that they are equal members of the team, that their input is welcomed and necessary, most students respond positively.

7 As a facilitator, how do I handle confidential issues that may arise during the SST?

The facilitator must be careful in handling confidential or other sensitive issues that emerge in the SST meeting. It is best to look at both verbal and non-verbal cues from the parent/guardian, and/or the student, to determine whether or not they are comfortable in pursuing a particular issue for discussion in front of the team gathered for the meeting. At times, it is useful to designate a member of the team to meet with the student or parent/guardian individually to discuss these issues. This separate meeting then becomes an action item listed in the SST Summary Form.

References

1   *The Search Institute*, Minneapolis, MN, n.d. www.search-institute.org
2   Project Cornerstone: Developmental Assets and Social and Emotional Learning, A YMCA of Silicon Valley Initiative, Santa Clara, CA, n.d.

School Attendance Review Team (SART)

Why Attendance Matters

School attendance is an integral component of student academic success. Regular school attendance is a necessary part of the learning and socialization process of children and youth. Poor attendance patterns can start as early as pre-school, and unless the underlying reasons are uncovered and addressed, the pattern can continue throughout the student's school career, can lead to academic failure and, in some cases, dropping out. While good attendance is largely a responsibility of the parents/guardians, and the student themselves, it is a job for which everyone shares a responsibility.

A high school diploma is seen by most as an important benchmark of our increasingly complex society. We have a serious problem in the United States with tens of thousands of students being truant from school every day, and many hundreds of thousands dropping out each year. The following quote is a sad commentary on the ongoing problem.

> Every September, approximately 3.5 million young people in America enter the eighth grade. Over the succeeding four years, more than 505,000 of them drop out—an average of 2,805 per day of the school year. Picture this: Every single school day, more than 70 school buses drive out of America's schoolyard, filled with students who will not return.
>
> [1]

Former President Barak Obama said the following:

> The dropout problem is one we cannot afford to ignore. The stakes are too high—for our children, for our economy, for our Country. The good news is, it doesn't have to be this way. We can have the courage to change. We can make a difference.

DOI: 10.4324/9781003240266-4

We can remember that these kids are all our kids. We will all profit, or pay for, whatever they become.

[2]

It is crucial that every school make the attendance of its students a priority, and make a committed effort to address the issues preventing students from regular school attendance.

In addition to serving individual students, the School Attendance Review Team (SART) promotes positive attendance practices within the school, and encourages all students to attend school on a regular basis. When positive school attendance is not being achieved, either school-wide or for individual students, the SART team uses a cycle of inquiry, including a review of the available data, the better to understand and address any and all issues that might be contributing to the problem(s).

Roles of the Student Attendance Review Team (SART)

* Assess, and continuously improve the positive attendance program and practices of the school.
* Keep a log of various interventions and dates that have been undertaken on behalf of a student, or a group of students.
* Send notifications of truancy to the home of the student(s).
* Invite parent(s)/guardian(s) into the school to meet with members of the SART.
* If the SART is expecting a caregiver(s) for a meeting, a reminder/follow-up phone call should be made prior to the scheduled meeting to address any issues(s) that might contribute to their not being able to attend.
* Make home visits after a number of attempts to have the caregivers come to the school for a conference have not been successful.
* Conduct meetings with parent(s)/guardian(s)/caregiver(s) that should result in a signed contract between the school, the caregiver(s) and the student.
* Disaggregate school and district data to determine whether trends or patterns exist in the student population with regard to poor attendance. Data can be broken down by grade, courses, teachers, gender, ethnicity, and under participation during distance learning.
* The SART should also consider the policies, practices and procedures of the school and school district, because they can contribute to the problems with poor attendance, or possibly students dropping out.
* Maintain documentation of the "conscientious effort" and the "due diligence" that have been undertaken before a student is considered for referral to the district/county level School Attendance Review Board (SARB). While most school districts have a SARB, not all cities have a truancy court that would be the last step if all other efforts taken to that point have not been successful.

The personnel who would/could serve on the SART

- The Attendance Technician/clerk who is most often the "backbone" of school attendance monitoring.
- Principal, Assistant Principal or Head Counselor/Dean.
- Counselor(s), especially when their student of record is being addressed.
- Student Welfare and Attendance liaison.
- School Nurse.
- School Social Worker.
- Special Education teacher if the student(s) they are responsible for is/are being discussed.
- School climate staff.
- Equity team staff.
- Dropout Prevention Specialist.
- Case manager(s) aka Care Coordinator(s).
- School Resource Officer, if one is assigned to the school.
- A representative from the Care Team with a particular expertise who can be called in to a SART meeting for specialized assistance.
- Partnership agency personnel.
- Others, as available and appropriate.

Key Considerations for an Effective Attendance Program

An effective attendance program [3] must be at the forefront of any school's program if it is to survive as a school. The mark of an effective attendance program can be measured by the school's ability and effectiveness in bonding students to the school, and within it, the staff, academic, extracurricular and social programs that the school offers. The following questionnaire has tried to identify and point out some of the multitude of factors that contribute to an effective program, or lack of same, at a school. These are good questions to ask the members of the team, or the entire faculty, about their attendance policies, practices and procedures.

Please answer yes or no to each of the following: Y= yes, N= no

1. Is good or improved attendance recognized and celebrated in the school?
2. Does our school have an effective attendance policy?
3. Are our attendance policy and practices clear to all personnel?
4. Does our school have a wide variety of extracurricular activities?
5. Is good attendance positively reinforced among the students?
6. Is good attendance positively reinforced among the staff?
7. Are students involved in decisions that affect them?

8. Does the climate and culture of our school enforce high expectations, good attendance and positive behavior?
9. Is our school environment welcoming and inviting to people from diverse cultures and backgrounds, and is as nurturing and stimulating as possible?
10. Does our school regularly examine attendance data, disaggregated by gender, ethnicity, English language learners, and special populations such as foster youth and unhoused students?
11. Are our attendance rates and numbers regularly communicated to staff, students and parents/guardians?
12. Does our school have the staff and resources to provide counseling around issues such as attendance?
13. Is there consistent, fair and equitable enforcement of all policies related to attendance for both staff and students?
14. Does our staff have opportunities for in-service activities that address issues such as parent communication, building relationships with students, teaching styles, cultural awareness, and classroom management?
15. Does our school have a functioning School Attendance Review Team (SART)?

Some Additional Considerations that Might be Impacting Attendance

1. Examine and reflect on whether the school-wide discipline practices are contributing to the poor attendance of some students.
2. Examine whether and how a negative school climate, even for some students, is contributing to their not feeling welcomed or supported.
3. Address any social dynamics, such as bullying, that is going on at the school.
4. Address gaps in learning due to missed learning opportunities, trauma at home, illness, chronic fatigue from irregular and inconsistent sleep patterns, and mental health issues, including addiction.
5. Inquire into the dynamics of relationships with teachers, and the dynamics in the classroom, and their possible contribution to the attendance problems seen in the student population.

A Multi-Tiered Approach to Attendance Improvement

Implementing a tiered approach to attendance is consistent with other efforts to provide student supports, and can be very useful to have implemented at the school site. Some examples are as follows:

Tier I: Universal Prevention Strategies

* Ensure that the classroom and school climate is safe and supportive for all students.
* Distribute information in multiple languages regarding the importance of school attendance.
* Ensure classroom environments are engaging to all students.
* Support teachers to discuss attendance patterns of their student in parent/ teacher conferences.
* Provide opportunities for students to contribute to their school community.
* Have high expectations that students attend school every day.
* Provide breakfast for all students, not just those with a certain eligibility. This addresses nutritional needs, and prepares the students for learning.
* Send information to parent(s)/guardian(s) regarding the relationship between attendance and achievement.
* Recognize good and improved attendance through classroom competitions, posting the names of students, and awarding certificates to students who have improved their attendance, or achieved perfect attendance.
* Ensure that student attendance data are accurately and routinely monitored.

Tier II: Early Intervention

* Assign an older peer ("buddy") to connect with the student to help getting them to school in the morning.
* Utilize SART meetings and conferences to create a support plan that addresses any barriers to regular attendance.
* Address any family stressors and barriers/hardships that are preventing the student from getting to school.
* Obtain the email addresses, and cell phone numbers from parents/guardians of their students to provide regular attendance updates.
* Check-In/Check-Out provides a familiar face every day, a person to connect with; and reinforces relationships/school connectedness.
* Provide access to parent liaisons that match parents culturally and linguistically to help facilitate home-school communication.
* Provide tutorial assistance if the student needs help with a particular subject or skill.
* Consider using a core group of students to reach out to and engage students who are socially isolated.
* At the conclusion of a SART conference, a contract is developed with defined responsibilities for the school, the caregiver(s) the student, and any other appropriate program and service providers.

* Provide referral assistance to services, programs and resources of the school, the district, and in the larger community.
* Contact the caregivers with "good news" when the student is showing improvement in his/her attendance.

Tier III: Intensive Intervention

* Consider a daily or weekly "travel sheet" where each classroom teacher notes the student's attendance, classroom participation and homework completion. It is then sent home for parent/guardian signature and returned to the school.
* Assign a staff mentor to connect regularly with the student, including morning phone calls and rides to school, if indicated.
* Address any safety issues that are preventing the student from getting to school.
* Work to obtain a "case manager", either in the school or in a community agency, for intensive work with the student and his/her family.
* In some instances, there might be another setting where the student can find more success, such as a continuation school or opportunity type program.
* Consider referral to the District/County Student Attendance Review Board (SARB).
* Consider bringing in a Deputy District Attorney to meet with parents/guardians and school personnel to discuss and address the possible consequences of continued absence from school.

Where to Start?

If the SART pulls data from the student information system, the team can proactively identify students who need intervention/support with their attendance issues. It is useful if the district office (mainframe operators) can provide a monthly attendance report to each school team describing the percentage of attendance for each student (e.g., 90%–100%, 80%–90%, 70%–80%, 60%–70%, below 60%), the name of the counselor, and the number of class periods and days of excused or unexcused absence. This gives the team crucial information to work with, and helps them to decide which steps to take with each student. The SART should also be looking for possible patterns of absences (e.g., certain periods, certain classes or teachers, a time in the school day, or reports from local business and residents regarding young people out on the street or in cafes during school hours) that can help the team to decide what area of intervention they need to address.

For individual students, it is useful if the SART keeps a *spreadsheet* that lists the various efforts undertaken. This will allow the team to keep track of what and when a particular intervention was implemented with a particular student. Along the top of the spreadsheet there would be listed interventions such as:

- Notification of poor attendance/truancy letters 1, 2 and 3 sent.
- Teacher Input Forms received.
- Conference with caregiver(s).
- Contract developed.
- Home visit.
- SST held.
- Follow-up on contract.
- Other supportive services provided.

Inviting Parent(s)/Guardian(s) to a SART Conference

Parents and guardians need to be informed of the meeting, along with the specifics of when, where, and some general information about why the SART is meeting regarding their child/student. They should also be given the contact information for a person they can speak with if there is a complication causing the need to re-schedule, and/or to answer any questions about the process.

Notification of the SART meeting can be sent home in a variety of ways:

- A letter sent home through ordinary mail.
- A letter sent home with registered mail, return receipt requested.
- A letter sent home with the student.
- A home visit for the most severe absences.

Getting the parents or guardians to the SART meeting might present a challenge, particularly because this is a not a "good news" meeting for them to attend, or else they might be somewhat complicit in the problem. Personal outreach by a member of the SART can go a long way in getting the caregivers to attend the meeting by addressing any real barriers or resistances they may have.

Involving the Non-Custodial Parent

As previously stated, trying to involve the absent parent can be very important. It is not uncommon to learn that a student frequently missing school is angry and disappointed by the absent parent for promises made and not kept, or ongoing conflict between the biological parents that can put the youngster in the middle of a "power struggle", or by being given different messages from each parent. When the non-custodial parent can become more involved in monitoring their youth's attendance, and spends regular time with their offspring, this can become a powerful incentive for the student to do better in school. Youngsters want people in their lives who can feel proud of them. It might be necessary to remind each parent that even though they are divorced or separated, and there is "bad blood" between them, they still share the heritage of the student who needs both of them in their lives.

The Tone of SART Conferences

This might be the first time the SART has had an opportunity to meet with the parent(s)/guardian(s), caregiver(s) of a student, and possibly the first time they have met with representatives of the school. It provides an opportunity to develop a collaborative relationship with them, and the rapport and cooperation that will be necessary to build a solid foundation for the student's future success. The SART, much like the SST process, is not into blaming or punitive approaches. If needed, some legal measures will come later if everything tried has not been successful. We want to be a partner with the family, and our hope is to have continued communication and cooperation with them as we both monitor and work to address the attendance concerns of the student. Good relationships between school representatives and the student's caregivers, along with the range of interventions considered, recommended and implemented, can make a significant difference in the improvement and subsequent success of the student.

The Flow of the Meeting

1. Start the meeting by having each of those gathered to introduce themselves along with their role/position, including the student and their parents/guardians.
2. Thank the parents/guardians for coming to the meeting.
3. Give an overview of the purpose of the meeting. Let the parents/guardians know that our goal is to work with them as a partner in the best interest of their student. Let them know that if the student is not in school, they won't be able to progress in their education toward eventual graduation.
4. Share the data of the student including unexcused and excused period or daily absences, current grades in progress, the scholarship record, and any documented behavioral issues.
5. Clearly state whether the student is on-track toward graduation.
6. The following are key questions for the student:
    * What was causing you to miss school, or certain periods or classes?
    * When was the last time you were successful in school?
    * Who supports you?
    * When you miss school, where are you?
    * What were you thinking at the time?
    * What/who has been impacted by you missing school? In what way?
    * Have you ever tried to improve your attendance, and what were the results?

- What can you do to improve your attendance?
- What do you think we can do together to improve your attendance?

7. Similarly, we might ask the parents/caregiver(s) the following questions:
   - What are your child's strengths, talents and interests?
   - Describe the reasons that you believe your child is missing school days.
   - Has attendance been a concern in previous years?
   - What have you tried so far to improve your child's attendance?
   - With whom at the school are you working to improve your child's attendance?
   - What/who has been impacted by your child's absences?
   - What can you do to help restore your student's good attendance?
   - How can we work together to improve your student's attendance?

The ultimate goal is to reintegrate the student back into good standing and regular attendance. A restorative and positive tone will help achieve this goal with the student and their caregiver(s).

- Let everyone know that there might be a need for a follow-up meeting, or phone call/email contacts, particularly if there is little or no improvement.
- Remind the student that they have a responsibility for their own education, and for the parent(s)/guardian(s) to fulfill their responsibility to ensure the regular attendance of their youngster.
- Everyone should sign the contract, defining the responsibilities of the school to the student, the student to his/her own education, and the parent(s)/guardian(s) to their student.
- A copy of the signed contract is given to each participant.
- Everyone should be thanked for participating in the SART meeting.

Identifying and Addressing the Root Causes of Absenteeism

Establishing a collaborative relationship with students and their caregivers will create an environment where the parties can work together to discover the root causes of the absenteeism/truancy.

Chronic absenteeism and truancy are most often symptoms of larger underlying causes. Like previously discussed, we like to call this the "uncovering" process, or "peeling the onion", as if going through the exterior layers further down to the core. The causes and solutions can be quite complex and often interrelated. At times there might be more than one challenge or barrier that the student and/or family are experiencing. The following additional questions can help in making sure the school site understands the root causes of the absenteeism.

* Have we discussed all of the reasons why your child has missed school?
* Are there any other reasons for the absences that we have not yet discussed?

School site SART meetings should work to address the underlying causes of the absences by providing any necessary services and supports. A meeting that does not end with the discussion and provision of services and support(s) will be far less effective because the source of the underlying reasons for the absenteeism might remain unresolved. Helping the caregivers to "bridge" to a particular agency or provider can help them to take advantage of that resource. "Bridging" can take the form of giving them the name and contact information for a particular person, or, in some cases, bringing a representative of a particular agency or resource to the school to meet with the caregivers on the school site. This would obviously be a follow-up action that is agreed upon at the SART meeting. A follow-up phone call to the caregiver(s) to determine whether they have connected with a particular agency or resource that was part of the SART contract can be very useful. If indicated, the school representative can assist them in addressing any barriers to following through.

Effective Use of SART Contracts

SART meetings will typically result in an agreement between the student, caregiver(s) and the school by developing a contract. Like any good contract, the SART contract should clearly state the terms and expectations to and from all of the parties. Ideally, everything discussed and agreed during a SART conference will be directly stated in the SART contract. This will help to avoid any ambiguity and provide a quick reference for all involved with regard to what is to be done, by whom, and when this particular item is to be implemented. Before the SART meeting ends, a member of the school team should verbally review the contract terms, and should explain each of the terms to avoid any confusion. Before inviting anyone to sign a contract, school staff should ask students and their caregiver(s) whether they understand the terms of the contract and answer any questions that arise. (A sample SART contract can be found in the SART Appendix).

The School Environment and its Policies, Practices and Procedures as Contributing Factors

While most of this Chapter has focused so far on individual students who are missing school, or are chronically truant, it is important to consider systemic factors that might be contributing to the problem. The school and/or the school system can significantly contribute to attendance problems in ways such as:

* A negative climate and culture of the school.
* A large, impersonal school that lacks supports and accommodations for students.
* The lack of a comprehensive orientation program for new students.
* A rigid schedule that does not allow students to repeat failed courses, and the school or district does not offer opportunities for credit recovery.
* Lack of positive, cooperative relationships among students, staff, parents and administrators.
* Negative disciplinary actions that are not consistently enforced among all students, and/or where the consequences are overly harsh relative to the actions on the part of the student, and not considered fair.
* Perceived negative messages from the school causing students to feel the school is not a welcoming environment for them.

Of interest is the Iowa Department of Education [4] which undertook a study back in 1989 to determine whether there were systemic policies and practices that were contributing to student failure and students dropping out of school. They looked at six different areas that may be negatively affecting student performance, especially in grades 7–12. The six areas were: Instruction, discipline, support services, attendance, student activities and school/community relations. They identified 45 specific areas that were causing problems for students, and listed 112 alternatives to address these identified areas. One practice they found particularly troubling was punishing student truancy by issuing out-of-school suspensions or lowering grades. They correctly stated that this practice pushes students out of school, creates a feeling of not belonging, and establishes a posture that the opportunity to learn will be taken away rather than fostered. The alternatives they recommended included providing reasonable consequences for truancy violations, providing opportunities to make up work by attending Saturday school, evening or an early bird program, and to reward academic achievement and behavior separately.

We believe that if other states, districts and schools would take a serious look at their policies, practices and procedures, they would also find some or many that are contributing to and reinforcing the attendance problems in their institutions.

Due Diligence and Documentation

If the school district and city/county government has a structure and process in place to hear cases when the work of the SART has not been successful, the matter is referred to the next step. In some communities this next step/structure is called the School Attendance Review Board (SARB), a last attempt at providing positive interventions prior to sending the matter to the District Attorney, that is if a particular community has a Truancy Court.

What is crucial if a matter gets to this level, is that there is evidence of the "due diligence" that has occurred and documented prior to being referred to either the SARB or the Truancy Court, as the Court will definitely want to see the documentation.

Home Visiting Tips

Although we would generally prefer that caregivers come to the school and participate in the SST or SART meeting process, there are times when a home visit might be indicated. Either due to resistance, or possibly some real barriers to their coming to the school, this option does not seem workable. A home visit can be very helpful in gaining a better understanding of the student, in the context of his/her living situation, and their relationship to their caregivers.

We are all aware that there are some neighborhoods that are less then safe, and each person will have to think about the risks and potential benefits of making a venture to the home. One rule of thumb is not to go alone, but to join with another member of the student support team if at all possible. A male/female team would be great if those personnel are part of the team.

Once inside the residence, or standing outside the door if the caregiver(s) is/are hesitant to allow you in, clearly state the concerns of the school about their youth's poor attendance and lack of success in school. State that you would like to work with them to improve the situation. Give them an opportunity to ask questions, to share their perspective on the causes of the concerns raised by the school, and listen to what they believe might be helpful, including what role they can take in a plan of success. The main purpose of the home visit is to try to engage the caregiver in a working relationship, and build a sense of trust that would allow a partnership on behalf of the student.

Before going out to the home, consider any cultural and/or language issues that would present a barrier if you are not prepared. In some families, the primary person to relate to is the mother, in others, the father, or other important people that are part of the extended family. Once in the home please consider the following:

* If refreshment is offered, accept it. In many cultures it is perceived as an insult not to accept an offer of hospitality such as this. The "breaking of bread" has an important symbolic meaning.
* Be prepared to answer questions which they have of you in the initial part of the interview. Don't be defensive, even if a personal question is asked, such as "Do you have children?". These attempts to "check you out" are generally to determine if you can be trusted with their personal insights and information. Even if their questions seem somewhat hostile, try not to be personally offended.
* A negative attitude may reflect previous bad experiences with educators and agencies, or reflect the general frustration of trying to cope with their child's issues. Allow or encourage ventilation if you perceive it may be necessary before moving

on to other issues. No matter what kind of person you are, in their eyes you are a representative of the school, the school district, "the system". It might be difficult for them to start working again with a new person or team from the school, particularly if there has been a lack of articulation and continuity with others they worked with previously. Keep the focus on the shared goal of helping the child/student to be more successful, by addressing whatever is "getting in the way".

* Throughout our work with the parent(s)/guardian(s), we are always trying to strengthen the natural relationship between them and their child. We are willing to share the "burden" of addressing the issues with them, but allowing too many of the responsibilities to be shifted to us will only weaken the alliance we are trying to build.

Strategies for Improving Student Attendance

* Raise the awareness of school personnel, parents, guardians, caregivers, community partners, and local businesses to the effects of chronic absence and truancy.
* Ensure that all schools record and post attendance period by period and on a daily basis.
* Identify and respond to grade level and pupil subgroup patterns of chronic absence and truancy.
* Identify and address factors contributing to chronic absenteeism and habitual truancy, including suspension and other disciplinary actions.
* Ensure that pupils with attendance problems are identified as early as possible in order to provide appropriate support services and interventions.
* Fully utilize school district software to compile accurate attendance data, produce daily reports and track the interventions provided to truant students.
* Inform parents/guardians and caregivers of the school district's method of verification of absences due to illness.
* Telephone or e-mail parents/guardians and caregivers in the early morning or early evening (dinner time) to notify them of the absences, and request a response to verify.
* Use bi-lingual aides to contact parent/guardians and caregivers with limited English ability and send out attendance notifications in the language appropriate to the family.
* Ensure the classroom and school climate is safe and supportive for all students.
* Have high expectations for students to attend school every day, and communicate this message to students and families.
* Provide schools with a pro-rata share of funds generated from improved attendance.
* Address chronic absenteeism rates during the transitions from elementary to middle schools, and from middle school to high school.

* Identify the specific school attendance barriers faced by children in poverty, foster youth, unhoused youth, and other significant populations with high chronic absenteeism rates.
* Address the problem of chronic absences, even when the absences have been excused.
* Develop attendance incentive programs.
* Ensure that all schools have an operational School Attendance Review Team (SART).
* Seek small or large financial incentives from the parent association to be awarded to the classroom with the best attendance record; allow teachers to spend the financial rewards for any purpose selected by the class members.
* Display attendance graphs in prominent locations to show current attendance goals and comparisons between past and present school year performance.
* Award students with improved or perfect attendance with a certificate or T-shirt.
* Hold a drawing for special prizes donated from local businesses. Use perfect attendance as the eligibility for the drawing.
* Publicize perfect attendance rewards in the local newspaper.
* Send commendation letters to students and caregivers for perfect or improved attendance.
* Ask teachers to emphasize the importance of regular school attendance when they meet with parents/guardians.
* Elicit the cooperation of doctors and dentists, and other allied health professionals, in scheduling appointments after school.
* Establish homeroom periods in secondary schools, with students remaining with the homeroom teacher for all four years of high school. Request that homeroom teachers monitor their students' attendance, and discuss truancy or chronic absenteeism with parent/guardians, or caregivers.
* Incorporate values clarification awareness into classroom instruction.
* Initiate a Student of the Month program that attempts to award this distinction to a student not normally in the mainstream of social activities, but who deserves needed recognition.
* Encourage staff to mentor students with poor attendance and related academic failure.
* Initiate make-up classes on one day of the weekend for pupils who have missed.
* Enlist the business community to provide mentors for frequently absent students and other indicators of being "at risk" for school failure.
* Initiate a "cross-age-helper" or "buddy" system in which older students with good attendance are permitted to assist younger students on a regular basis. Another possibility is for the "buddy" to call the younger student in the morning and, if they live close by, to walk/ride with them to school.
* Personalize relationships between pupils and attendance office personnel, clerks, custodians or secretaries to make individual contact with chronic absentees on a regular basis.

- Increase efforts to create public awareness of attendance problems in the community through newspaper articles and public service announcements on radio and television.
- Solicit local businesses to provide free promotional coupons to students with perfect attendance.
- Conduct school-wide orientation assemblies at the beginning of the school year. These assemblies can help students understand the complexities of secondary schools in particular, familiarize them with the policies and procedures of the school, and where supportive services are available.
- Make home visits concerning student absences if parents/guardians cannot be contacted through other means, or are unable or unwilling to come to the school.
- Calculate and publicize unearned daily attendance funds from unexcused absences.
- Whenever possible, involve both mothers and fathers in addressing the attendance issue.
- Refer students/families to appropriate district and community resources and services to address issues related to school attendance. This is particularly important if the caregivers are somehow complicit in contributing to the poor attendance.
- For Special Education students, write attendance goals and supports into the IEP.
- Use retired community volunteers to provide tutorial services to students who show at-risk patterns of poor attendance and academic failure.
- Set up group counseling or small group guidance seminars for students with poor attendance.
- Provide mentoring relationships to students with poor attendance.
- Provide parent/guardian education classes/discussion classes/discussions to help them provide and support regular attendance in their youngsters.
- Distribute a small card, similar to the size of a business card, that provides the school's answering service number and directions for reporting absences.
- Help to ensure a District/County level School Attendance Review Board.
- For students who have already dropped out, reach out and re-engage them into a viable educational program.

SART Frequently Asked Questions

1   What is the purpose/goal of a School Attendance Review Team (SART)?

The overall goal of the SART is to improve the attendance of students at the school site. First and foremost, the SART implements positive attendance practices in the school for all staff and students. The SART should also recognize those students who improve their attendance via charts, interclass competition, or prizes. In order for the SART to do its job, teachers must record attendance, both daily and period by period, without fail. This is the only way to ensure accuracy of the data for the SART to utilize.

The SART is also empowered to notify parents/guardians of any unexcused absences, excessive "excused" absences, including excessive absences "excused" due to "illness". This is usually done through Notification of Absence letters, typically letters 1, 2 and 3, as indicated, if the problem continues. Usually, the second letter requires the parent(s)/ guardian (s) and the student to attend a meeting with a member(s) of the SART. These meetings /conferences attempt to address the reasons for the poor attendance and develop a contract with the parent/guardian and the student. This contract needs to be monitored regularly. If the absences continue, the SART will send a third and possibly a fourth notification that declares the student as a "habitual truant". If the truancy continues, a third letter will typically ask for another conference with the student and caregiver(s) in another effort to resolve the issues causing the truancy.

If the student does not improve his/her attendance, the team will decide if the matter should be referred to the Student Attendance Review Board, a district/city level structure that will also work to determine the causes or the continued truancy, and to develop an agreement/contract with specific actions that must be implemented. After the school and district has made a conscientious effort to work with the student and family, and these efforts have still not been successful, the SARB will prepare documentation to refer the matter to the local District Attorney who will put the matter on the truancy court calendar, if a truancy court calendar exists in your community. At that point, the judge has a number of options that s/he can impose at their discretion.

2   We have so many students at our school, how can we keep track of so many with poor attendance histories?

All school districts have recording and tracking information devices for student attendance. Most of them will have to report that information to their respective states on a regular basis in order to obtain funding based on the number of students attending in the school district. Often called the "mainframe", the technicians can print out data that will provide very valuable information to the SART. For each student, the number of days missed, excused or unexcused, tardiness, and class periods missed. The data might also show irregular patterns that indicate class "cutting". A high school where one of us worked received regular reports from the main office with the names of students by the percentage of time they were attending, and grouped by the names of their counselors. There were students attending 90%–100% of the time, 80% to 90%, 70% to 80%, 60% to 70%, and those below 60%. The counselor would be the first person to do what they could to improve the attendance and if needed, participate with other members of the SART in a conference with parents/ guardians and the student.

It is useful if the SART creates a spreadsheet to track their efforts on behalf of the student. Various "interventions" are listed at the top of the spread sheet and the names of students down the side of the document. There would be a place to check off when a certain intervention has occurred. Items listed might include: Phone call to parent, the date that letters 1, 2 and 3 were sent, contract signed, home visit, SST held, or service referrals made.

3   Who should make up the members of SART?

A team would typically be made up of a chair/facilitator, a counselor(s)/head counselor, Dropout Prevention Specialist (DPS), clerical staff at the school responsible for attendance, school social worker, dean or head counselor, a school resource officer if one is serving at the school, and possibly a member of a school-based or school-linked agency that provides services to the student and his/her family. In some cities, Juvenile Probation officers are assigned to school areas so they can attend SART meeting and monitor their wards at the school site. (Possible members of the SART are also listed in the main section of this chapter describing the SART).

4   When can our SART meet?

Much like the Care Team and the Student Success Team (SST), the SART members need to be very flexible to find times to meet. Most of the SART personnel typically do not have classroom responsibilities, and hopefully they can work out a time that is convenient for the majority of them. When a particular parent/guardian is coming in for a conference, all other members of the SART should be notified so they can decide whether they should attend the conference for a particular student.

5   What are some questions that will help the student to open up at the SART conference?

* What happened to make you miss school?
* What were you thinking about at the time?
* Who has been impacted by your missing school? In what way?
* What can you do to improve your attendance?
* What do you think we can do together to improve your attendance?

6   What are some questions that will help the caregiver(s) to open up at the SART conference?

* What happened to lead your son/daughter to miss school?
* What was your thought process when you learned of it?
* Who has been impacted by your child's absences? In what way?
* What can you do to restore your student's good attendance?
* What do you think we can do together to improve your student's attendance?

References

1   Smink, Jay, and Schargel, Franklin, *Helping Students Graduate: A Strategic Approach to Dropout Prevention*, Larchmont, NY, Eye on Education, 2004, page 9.

2   Comments made by President Barak Obama at the Launch of My Brother's Keeper Alliance, Lehman College, West Bronx, New York, May 4, 2015.

3   Gonzales, Luis D., The Prevention of Truancy: Programs and Strategies That Address the Problems of Truancy and Dropouts, Los Angeles County Office of Education, Division of Evaluation, Attendance and Pupil Services, n.d.

4   Inventory of Policies and Practices Related to Student Failure and Dropping Out, Iowa Department of Education, 1989.

5 Meeting Facilitation

The Role of the Facilitator and Facilitation

Experience has shown that the manner in which an SST or SART meeting is facilitated has a direct relationship to the outcome of the meeting, either positive or negative, as well as affecting what they are able to accomplish, or not.

Facilitation is an art that takes a lot of practice. Getting up in front of a number of people who have a relationship to the student can be anxiety provoking. It involves exposure of one's skills, or lack of same; but it can become a very powerful skill, if practiced and developed. The first and foremost role of the facilitator is to make sure that all of those gathered for an SST, or other team process meeting, are comfortable and understand the process that will be followed, and that they understand that the input of everyone is welcomed, encouraged and respected, particularly if they are the caregiver(s), and/or the student who is the focus of the meeting.

The facilitator is actually a *guide* through the discussion process. S/he is not necessarily described as a "leader" but the one who keeps the discussion on track. The facilitator does not initially include his or her own thinking, but rather works to draw out the items relevant to the discussion from the assembled group. There are times when the facilitator needs to refocus the group in order to keep the discussion on track and consistent with the SST Summary, or other form of group memory.

The following process points are useful for the facilitator to keep in mind in order for the meeting flow to unfold in a positive direction.

1. The facilitator asks staff and family members to introduce themselves and their relationship to the student.
2. The facilitator explains the purpose and process of the SST or SART meeting, including the time frame for the meeting.

DOI: 10.4324/9781003240266-5

3. The facilitator ensures that the strengths of the student are the first discussion item. Starting with the strengths sets a positive tone for the meeting, and gives everyone an opportunity to be heard, thus setting the stage for equal input and respectful listening.
4. The facilitator should guide the meeting along, being mindful of the time, and the importance of keeping the tone positive.
5. If an SST meeting, the facilitator works to ensure that the discussion process closely follows the columns listed on the SST "header", or other form of "group memory".
6. Student and caregiver(s) input is sought within the first ten minutes of the meeting. The facilitator works to ensure that a broad range of interventions is considered: The classroom, larger school/district, home and the community.
7. The facilitator works to ensure that everyone's input is sought during the "brainstorming" section that will lead to the defined action items.
8. Before finalizing the action items, the facilitator reads them to the group to ensure consensus.
9. The facilitator ensures that the responsibility (Who) for each action item is assigned, a completion date (When) agreed, and a follow-up meeting date determined.
10. The facilitator ensures that everyone signs the Actions document developed to show that they have participated in the meeting.
11. The facilitator thanks everyone for their participation, and restates the date for the follow-up meeting.

Key Concepts of Facilitation

Facilitation is a way of providing leadership without taking the reins. The job of the facilitator is to get others to assume responsibility with their thoughts, ideas and commitments.

1. The facilitator stays neutral on content. S/he focuses on the process. This doesn't mean that you, as the facilitator, can't offer suggestions; it just means that you shouldn't impose your opinions on the topic before the group.
2. The facilitator actively listens. S/he actively listens, and should look people in the eye, using positive body language.
3. The facilitator asks questions, tests assumptions, invites participation, and gathers information.
4. The facilitator paraphrases to clarify (e.g., "are you saying", "What I'm hearing you say is…")
5. The facilitator encourages the team to synthesize ideas. S/he gets people to comment on what others are saying, and build on them, if appropriate.
6. The facilitator helps/guides the team to stay on track. S/he sets a time frame for the meeting, and appoints a timekeeper.

7. The facilitator can create a "parking lot" to record ideas that are important but not on the topic at the time they are brought up, and will be revisited later in the discussion process.

8. The facilitator regularly evaluates the effectiveness of the meeting by eliciting feedback from the group members. S/he calls on people who seem to be disengaged from the process.

9. The facilitator brings assumptions out into the open to clarify them, and challenge them, if it is indicated.

10. The facilitator keeps track of emerging ideas and final decisions. Notes should reflect what people actually said and not the facilitator's interpretation of what was said.

11. The facilitator helps the team to identify next steps, identify action items, and determine who is responsible and when tasks are to be accomplished.

Facilitation Skill Practice

The best way to hone your skills as a facilitator is to have your peers critique your performance. The Facilitator Assessment Checklist is used to get feedback from others who have been asked by you for their honest assessment in the interest of improvement. As previously said, the "art" of facilitation doesn't come naturally or easily to most of us, and it does take practice to be able to become more proficient in the "art". Those who assume the role of observer need to have your best interest at heart, just as you will have when you, in turn, observe them. This is the kind of teamwork that can help to make each of us better at effectively serving the children and youth. The facilitator regularly evaluates the effectiveness

Facilitation Assessment Checklist [1]

Behaviors that Help	Behaviors that Hinder
_____ listens actively	_____ oblivious to group needs
_____ maintains eye contact	_____ no follow-up on concerns
_____ helps identify needs	_____ poor listening
_____ gets buy-in	_____ strays into content
_____ surfaces concerns	_____ loses track of key ideas
_____ defines issues	_____ makes poor notes
_____ brings everyone into the discussion	_____ ignores conflicts
_____ uses good body language	_____ provides no alternative for structuring the discussion
	(Continued)

Behaviors that Help	Behaviors that Hinder
_____ paraphrases continuously	____ gets defensive
_____ provides useful feedback	____ puts people down
_____ accepts and uses feedback	____ doesn't paraphrase
_____ checks time and place	____ lets a few people dominate
_____ monitors and adjusts the process	____ never asks "How are we doing?"
_____ asks relevant probing questions	____ tries to be center of attention
_____ keeps an open attitude	____ lets the group get sidetracked
_____ stays neutral	____ projects a poor image
_____ is optimistic and positive	____ uses negative or sarcastic tone
_____ manages conflict well	____ talks too much
_____ takes a problem-solving approach	____ doesn't know when to stop
_____ stays focused on the process	
_____ looks calm and present	**Additional Observations**
_____ skillfully summarizes what is said	_____

Reference

1 Bens, Ingrid M., *Facilitation at a Glance: A Pocket Guide of Tools and Techniques for Effective Meeting Facilitation*, Methuen, Maine, GOAL/QPC, 2008.

6 | The Benefits of Effective Teaming

When approaching a new task, such as serving on a student support team, most people experience anxieties and apprehensions about how effectively they will be able to perform in this challenging role. Working as a team member often involves change in traditional ways of working, and the loss of what are perceived as the advantages of working alone. It involves sharing with others, and it can be both physically and emotionally draining. It requires giving up a certain amount of "territorial imperatives", and it involves exposure. Although these anxiety producing elements are to be understood and respected, all of them have been experienced and successfully overcome by many others.

Nothing speaks better than success itself to counteract initial misgivings. As the team proceeds with its work, the awareness of improved communication, shared responsibility, and mutual support can serve to generate a sense of togetherness and purpose. By proceeding in their work with students, staff and parents/guardians, and by observing the positive effects that can be achieved, team members can renew in themselves a sense of mastery and success in their work. Team efforts can and do bring the same satisfaction we hope our youngsters will achieve as they overcome their own anxieties and roadblocks to mastery. In addition to the positive effects experienced by the staff, the effect of coordinated planning and intervention can have a profound effect for the child/student and his or her family.

Efforts at "teaming" skills and sharing efforts can provide that preventive and early intervention thrust that is necessary to bring about success for the student. In addition, Student Support Team efforts create a structure in which those who need additional services in order to achieve their potential can be identified, screened and addressed.

DOI: 10.4324/9781003240266-6

Terms Applicable to "teamed efforts"	Terms that may be applicable to "un-teamed" efforts
Coordinated	Uncoordinated
Integrated	Disintegration
Interdependency	Vacuum
Shared support	Fragmented
Support network	Isolation
Can lead to: Improved functioning	Can lead to: Dysfunction

The Characteristics of an Effective Team

To be effective, a team must:

* Have a clear understanding of its goals.
* Have achieved a high degree of communication and understanding among its members.
* Be able to initiate and carry out effective decision-making, carefully securing the commitment of all members.

Things People Like About Teams/Committees when they Function Well

* The role of the committee is clearly defined (i.e., what the committee and its members are supposed to do and what their goals are).
* Time is carefully controlled. Meetings start on time and end on time. Enough time is allowed to complete the work.
* Team members are sensitive to each other's needs and expressions. People listen to and respect others' opinions.
* Meetings are conducted in an informal relaxed atmosphere rather than in a more formal exchange pattern.
* The chairperson and committee members are well briefed. Materials are prepared and available.
* Members are all qualified and interested. They want to be part of the committee. A definite commitment exists.
* Interruptions are avoided, or held to a minimum.
* Good minutes and records are kept so that decisions are not lost.
* Periodically, the committee stops and assesses its own performance. Needed improvements are worked out.

* Team members feel they are given some kind of reward for their efforts. Recognition and appreciation are given so that they feel they are really making a contribution.
* The work and recommendations of the team are accepted and utilized, and can make a significant impact to the school.

Reasons Why People Do Not Like to Serve on Teams/Committees

* The leadership is poor. The leader fails to keep the discussion on the subject, to monitor and direct discussion to keep things moving in the appropriate direction, or to engage in those activities that are stimulating and motivating to the members.
* The goals are unclear. Members are not sure what they are trying to accomplish (i.e., What are we supposed to be doing today?").
* Assignments are not taken seriously by committee members. There is an apparent lack of commitment.
* Recommendations of the committee are often ignored by the top administration. The administration needs to be more responsive to the team/committee.
* Meetings are considered a waste of time. Discussions of concerns are unproductive, with no direction, conclusions or decisions.
* There is a lack of follow-through with assignments on the part of the team members.
* Often one person or a clique dominates. Some members talk and push for their position, trying to exclude the views of others.
* Members get into discussions that only a couple of them think are important, causing the entire discussion to steer off track.
* Committee members are unprepared, including the chairperson of the meeting. The agenda is not ready, and materials and other things that really need to be at the table are not available. Someone has not done his or her homework.
* No action is taken. The committee spends a lot of time in discussion without coming up with specific items that lead to action.
* People often have hidden agendas—personal "axes" to grind.

Supporting and Serving Special Populations

Unhoused Students

* Unhoused students often suffer from common chronic illnesses such as asthma, diabetes and dental problems, causing them to miss school. Remedy: Connect homeless students to school nurses and provide the nurses with the resources to implement Nurse Case Management principles to improve the attendance of such students.
* Unhoused students undergo markedly more trauma than their housed peers, and experience higher rates of anxiety and depression. Solution: Connect homeless students with school social workers, counselors, or an outside therapist for support.
* Host regular, small group lunch meetings where students can talk with each other about school, relationships, goals and challenges.
* Unhoused students sometimes come to school without adequate supplies, or adequate hygiene, and are often subjected to bullying and embarrassment. Answer: Provide these students with hygiene kits, showers, clothing, access to a clothes washer/dryer, and needed school supplies. Either McKinney Vento funds or Title 1, Part A funds can be used for these needs when other community resources are not available.
* Many unhoused students miss school to care for younger siblings or to work. Countermeasure: Support working students by helping them to find jobs that are close to school and after school hours, possibly offering them a flexible school schedule.
* Help families find high-quality and affordable child care and other early childhood education programs in the area.
* Lack of timely transportation can contribute to absenteeism for students experiencing homelessness. For example, lack of timely transportation to medical appointments or jobs can result in students missing partial or full days of school. Some strategies include:
  1. Using ride-sharing options.
  2. Collaborating with medical transportation services that can be covered by students' or parents' Medicaid or other health insurance.

DOI: 10.4324/9781003240266-7

3. Working with community agencies and faith-based organizations that have vans to assist with transportation.

4. Providing pre-paid gas cards to parents or guardians of homeless students, if indicated.

5. Using data to build the case for increased transportation resources through McKinney-Vento funding.

- Build caring, supportive relationships both with students and families to help motivate daily attendance, address challenging barriers, and connect with students on their terms when they return from an absence.

- Provide positive reinforcement to influence behavior and attendance (e.g., celebrating good or improved attendance, reminders of coming to school, universal free breakfast programs, greeting and welcoming students at the school door).

- The Check and Connect program [1], which has shown success, utilizes a volunteer to build a trusting relationship between students and adult mentors, who commit to know and support the youth for at least two years.

- When students miss 20% or more of school days, collaborate with other agencies to intervene (housing agencies, child welfare, juvenile justice departments, and case management programs).

- Continue the child's or youth's education in the school of origin for the duration of their being unhoused.

- If the student has special education eligibility, provide input on the impact that changing schools had on the student's progress, and any services they are receiving. If a school change is indicated, ensure that evaluations and/or services are not interrupted.

Youth in Foster Care

- School staff should contact the youth's new caregiver, and social worker, to inform them of the youth's right to remain in their school of origin.

- Develop a conference call with members of the youth's support services team. This might include the Child Welfare Worker, Court Appointed Special Advocate (if the student has one), the foster parent, Educational Rights Holder (ERH), counselor/therapist, education advocate, counselor of the new school, or a rep from the youth's previous school. The purpose of this call would be for the various support personnel to get to know one another, to share strategies and insights regarding the youth, and exchange contact information.

- Work with the various members of the student support team to develop immediate and long-term educational plans for the student, ensuring that the student's education is not interrupted.

- Develop a transportation plan.

- When enrolling in a new school, assign/place the student in the least restrictive environment for his/her needs.
- Provide information on the commute to the schools under consideration in terms of distance, mode of transportation, and travel time, and work with appropriate case workers to develop transportation plans.
- Work with school staff and data managers to ensure appropriate confidentiality about the student's out-of-home placement.
- Consider the anticipated duration of the child's out-of-home placement and his or her permanency plan.

Re-Engagement of Youth who are Disengaged or Have Dropped Out

We would like to share with you our experience working to re-engage students who had formerly dropped out back into a viable educational option for them. A number of years ago Howard was awarded a federal dropout demonstration grant to work with students whom the district had listed as having dropped out. The team of seven "case managers" gathered the names, addresses and phone numbers of some 200 of these formerly enrolled students and, for evaluation purposes, a control group of 200 who were still in school. The first task was to find these youths and so, with phone numbers and addresses in hand, the case managers started to search for them. Somewhat to even our surprise, we were able to find nearly all of them. Almost to a person, they were glad we had come, as the majority of them had no idea of the educational options, programs and services that were available to them.

In our conversations with them, a majority of these young adults did not want to return to the same school they had dropped out from. They were, however, quite open to discussing what might be out there for them. The next step was to develop a working relationship with each of them that would endure over time. Once a relationship had been established, we had to get a sense of each youth's educational and personal needs so that we could collaboratively develop a service plan with them.

The options presented to these young adults included two site-based Re-Entry programs created to address credit deficiencies, courses failed, and other barriers that contributed to them dropping out. We also developed a transitional Back on Track small school. Other programs and resources of the school district and the larger community, such as General Equivalency Diploma (GED) programs and Community College, were also considered. At the end of our two-year program, we were able to show statistically that we were able to keep more of the former dropouts in an educational option than those in the control group.

The reason we are sharing this project with you is because as schools start to re-open after more than a year being closed, we believe there will be a significant number of students who will not be returning on their own. Some of these will be students who already had "one foot out the door" prior to the Pandemic, and this coupled with this lengthy period of being out of school, just tipped them over the edge. Others have not been participating in the on-line sessions, or their attendance has been very poor. Many students, even if they were given a computer by their school, did not have access to the internet and could not tune in even if they wanted to. Many believe that the instructional time lost for many students during the Pandemic will significantly increase the achievement gap. These students will need outreach in order to re-engage them into a viable educational option for them.

It is important that students who have been disengaged from school for some time need to be wholeheartedly welcomed back into the school. Our experience, working with students who have been absent for some time, is that they tend to be given a very lukewarm welcome, or in some cases, even negative statements once they return (i.e., "You have already failed this course."). A more positive welcome might be, "I can still give you some partial, or variable credit, even though you won't be able to earn full credit for this course.").

What can we do to assist the number of students who will not just walk back into our public schools on their own?

First, obtain the phone numbers and addresses of any and all students who have not returned to your school. Start by making a phone call to see if you can connect with the student and tell them it would be great if they could come in and meet with you to discuss their educational needs and goals, even if they don't want to come back to this particular school. After meeting with them, an informal assessment process can be done by reviewing historical data that will help both of you to decide where they might continue their education.

1. Keep a list of those students who do not answer or respond to messages from you. These are the ones who will require personal outreach such as a home visit, or possibly to a community location where young people are known to gather. Both are places that you might be able to connect with, and hopefully engage the previously enrolled, or still currently enrolled students.
2. When you meet with each youth talk to them openly about their perceptions of the issues that caused them to become disengaged, or dropped out.
3. Explore possible changes that may help the youth to view the teachers/school as supportive, and to perceive courses and other educational activities as personally valuable for them, and attainable.
4. Work to establish and maintain a working relationship so that ongoing interactions are designed to create a sense of trust, open communication, and to provide personalized support and direction.

5. Negotiate involvement in a viable educational setting through the development of mutual goals and agreements. The focus throughout this discussion is on clarifying an awareness of valued options, working to enhance their expectations of positive outcomes for themselves.

With regard to the school and the school system itself, there must be a good deal of thought about what will be necessary to re-engage students. This might require some staffing and other changes along with the development of new or additional programs. A range of programs and options should be in place for students based on their needs, as determined through interview, and review of records (transcripts, credits, attendance history). In some cases, working with a school psychologist to obtain baseline data through the use of psychometrics that are not utilized in formal assessments for Special Education may be in order, or classroom teachers doing informal assessments to get a sense of each student's needs.

We are of the opinion that many more students will fall by the wayside (dropout) if the school system is unable or unwilling to "meet them where they are at".

So, what would this so called "range of options" look like?

An individual student support professional cannot do this by himself or herself. It is very important that your school has site support teams in place and functioning, such as a School Coordinated Care Team (SCCT), a Student Success Team (SST) process and a School Attendance Review Team (SART). Many individual students will need the attention of one or more of these teams to plan the actions that will be necessary to re-integrate them successfully into school. Whether you are a facilitator of one of these teams, or a team member, you can advocate for the importance of these teams, as well as for a range of options for these teams to draw open in addressing student needs.

At the elementary level, many students will need some individual or small group instruction/remediation. Some will invariably need therapeutic services as well, particularly if a member of their immediate or extended family has died or suffered from the virus.

Most of the following ideas will relate to high schools; but middle schools will also need to have skill development options as well as therapeutic services. Based on what we know about individual students, there will be a need for some credit recovery options. Here are a few possibilities to make up course credit.

* Individual subject learning packets that students can complete on their own to make up a credit.
* Individual Small Group Instruction (ISGI), composed of a small group of students based on their skill needs working with a teacher or tutor.
* Teachers working with students after school to make up full or partial credit.
* After the school year ends, an intensive two-week program with core subject teachers to help the student(s) to show competency in the course material they have failed or did not complete. If the student can show a satisfactory level of competency to the teacher, they are given the credit for a course.

Re-Entry Program Models

There are students who need increased structure, monitoring and personalization to keep them on track. In this group are those who have not earned enough credits to be promoted from the ninth to the tenth grade. Others who have not participated, or done so in a very limited way, in the online learning, might need this type of structure or program.

a. **Student Support and Assistance Program: (SSAP)**
   * Students in this program take a first hour English "block" class that is co-taught by two SSAP teachers. The last 30 minutes of this class are enrichment.
   * The last class of the day is Algebra, which is taught by an SSAP teacher.
   * Check in is done twice a day.
   * Attendance is monitored by daily phone calls, home visits, and parent/guardian conferences.
   * Character education is provided that includes psycho-educational groups, a classroom guidance curriculum, and student portfolios. Social work and counseling services are available to support the program teachers.

b. **CORE Program**
   * Five teachers and a counselor/social worker agree to work together as a team. They agree to a common prep for planning and conferencing. They coordinate their strategies with individual students, something that is almost impossible in a traditional high school setting. Materials and lesson plans are shared and coordinated.
   * The students remain as a "core" group throughout the day in one classroom for all classes. The teachers leave their own classrooms and do the moving to the students rather than the other way around.
   * Counselor/social worker meet weekly with teachers to discuss students.
   * Parent/guardian conferences are held with all program staff during weekly meetings. Student attendance, progress and other concerns are addressed.
   * Communication and coordination within the team are strong components of the program.

c. **Mission Model**
   * For students returned to school after having dropped out, repeat ninth graders, and others who have fewer than 60 credits.
   * Students are interviewed by the program teacher(s) and a dropout prevention specialist/counselor.
   * The student is placed into three AM classes within the Re-Entry program (English, World Civilization and Math). This schedule can be modified if the student has already completed one or more of these courses/credits.
   * Variable credit is offered for these courses so that students can earn one credit at a time (based on a five unit per course model for each course), therefore helping the students to see some growth rather than passing or failing the entire course.

d. **Academic/Vocational Re-Entry program**
   - This program is housed in a technical/vocational high school.
   - Students attend three or four classes in the Re-Entry program in the morning, and take the vocational/technical classes in the afternoon.
   - The class is self-contained. Students stay with the same multi-credentialed teacher all morning.
   - Study skills and other high school success skills are integrated into the curriculum.

e. **Back on Track Program**
   - A one semester "back on track" transitional program for those students who are recovered from having dropped out, who are seriously disengaged, or whose attendance is so poor that returning to a comprehensive high school is unworkable.
   - The program (previously implemented in San Francisco Unified) was developed out of a need for students who felt they just could not go back, or "make it" in a comprehensive high school, particularly the one they had dropped out from. Possible choices for these students include a "transitional" program to return them to a comprehensive or continuation school, a GED program, preparation to take the high school proficiency exam, admission to an adult school or community college (depending on age), or other options that might be available in the larger community.
   - The program included five staff members: A program lead school social worker, two teachers, a counselor/work experience coordinator, and a case manager/activities coordinator.

f. **Continuation School and Job Corps Partnership Program**
   - Students attend a continuation school in the morning for core academics.
   - Students are then transferred to a Job Corps site in the afternoon for career preparation courses that can lead to apprenticeships in various unions. (Other arrangements for the division of time between the two systems might be necessary.)
   - Course credit toward high school graduation, as well as GED preparation, are both offered. Often the Job Corps Center does not offer certain courses that the district might, and the district might not provide those programs and experiences available at the Job Corps center.

Reference

1   PBIS Rewards, 2021, 223 NW 2nd Street, Evansville, IN 47708, Phone (812) 434–6685.

The Importance of School Climate and Culture

The truth is that every school has a climate. It is either developed—planned with intent—or is developed by proxy. When planned with positive intent, it can be supportive, protective, nurturing and conducive to effective teaching and learning. Unfortunately, when neglected, it can also be unsafe, unsupportive and disconnected. Imagine that you are a teacher, or a parent entering such a school on a daily or weekly basis. How would it make you feel, motivated or distracted, supported or vulnerable?

[1]

When going into a school, try to put yourself in the shoes of a student enrolled there. As the "student", do people acknowledge you and say "good morning", are there bulletin boards that celebrate diversity and recognize student achievements, is the building clean and inviting, do the teachers greet students at the door of their classrooms and invite them in? Is there a listing of opportunities, such as clubs and other activities for students to participate in? Do the teachers seem generally happy to be teaching at this school? Are the rules and expectations for students clearly stated and visible, and do the disciplinary practices seem fair and evenly enforced? These are some of the signs to look for in evaluating the culture and climate of the school.

Unfortunately, there are some schools that are considered "toxic", environments that make it difficult to learn in, or to teach in. Let's take a look at some significant negative (toxic) school climate indicators:

* A blend of negative expectations and pessimism regarding students.
* An attitude that there is nothing wrong with the school, there is merely an influx of inferior students.
* A philosophy of discipline based on fear, intimidation, coercion and punishment.
* A blatant disregard for student rights.
* A large measure of inattention and insensitivity to ethnic and racial concerns.

DOI: 10.4324/9781003240266-8

* An absence of any student involvement and input in any significant decision-making process.
* A rigid, unrealistic and sometimes punitive grading policy.
* A reward system that recognizes only a very narrow number of successes.
* A drab physical environment.

Some schools do not have a nurturing environment for either staff or students. This can significantly affect the work of the student support teams that are working with individual students in the context of this reality. Obviously if the school is toxic, it will be necessary to correct the toxicity of the school if one is to effectively assist the students who attend there.

The following is a quote from one such school:

> We had a poor curriculum, poor student-staff relationships, and no sense of "community togetherness". Most students did not feel like we were a family. For the sake of the students, we had to design a process for encouraging relationships of trust between students and staff. Students have difficulty learning until they connect with staff.
>
> [2]

The following is a School Climate Profile that can be used at your school site or district, and adapted as indicated. You might consider having the staff and faculty take this survey, see what comes up, and what can be learned from this exercise.

School Climate Inventory [3]

Legend: 1 = Almost never, 2 = Occasionally, 3 = Frequently, 4 = Almost always, 5 = Always

You can do this profile focusing on "what is" currently and "what should be"

1. Students are treated with respect by teachers.
2. Students can count on teachers to listen to their side of the story and to be fair.
3. Students feel enthusiastic about learning in this school and enjoy coming to school.
4. Staff enjoy working at this school.
5. I feel that my ideas will be listened to in this school.
6. Parents/guardians are considered by this school as important contributors.
7. Staff at this school are continually seeking ways to improve the educational system.
8. The school program is appropriate to students' present and future needs.
9. All staff work together to make the school run smoothly.
10. Students would rather be at this school than transfer to another.
11. Staff at this school would rather be at this school than transfer to another.

12. There is someone at this school upon whom I can rely.
13. The staff really cares about the students.
14. Each student's special abilities (intellectual, artistic, social or physical) are challenged.
15. Performance expectations are tailored to the individual student.
16. Students have opportunity for learning in individual, small group and classroom groups.
17. Teachers have a wide range of teaching materials and media.
18. The school's program encourages students to develop self-discipline and initiative.
19. Staff enforces the rules fairly.
20. The staff lets students know when they have done something particularly well.
21. Are there reasonable alternatives to out-of-school suspension in our school?
22. Are our students apprehensive about their own personal safety in the halls, the restrooms and lunch area?

School Climate and Culture in Relation to Students' Mental Health and Well-Being

Many students who come to the attention of a student support team are thought to be in need of mental (behavioral) health services. It is true that far too many children and youth are not getting the care and attention they need to address their internal stresses and difficulties. It is also true that in evaluating an individual student, it is important to look at the totality of experiences in their daily life both in school and elsewhere. Earlier in this book (Endnote 2 in Chapter 1) we quoted Ron Edmonds speaking about the power of the school to positively influence and overcome negative experiences in various environments.

We know that students enter our school with many different skill levels, personal needs, a diversity of "resiliency" traits, and motivation to succeed, as well as a range of supports at home and in the community. How effectively we meet them where they are, and how we assist them in addressing and enhancing these differing levels and needs, can have a profound impact on their entire lives.

No matter how much therapy a student might be getting in one or two hours a week provided either within or outside of the school, their life in school can be a contributing factor to a positive therapeutic effect for them, or counter therapeutic effect.

There is an important link between the climate and culture of the school, and a student's motivation to learn. We know that students who find strong social and emotional support in the school are much more likely to be successful academically, and they also have an enhanced sense of belonging and bonding to the school.

Our hope is for the school to be a "caring community" with many positive relationships, high expectations, and opportunities for young people to make a contribution to their community. To the extent that the climate of the school is one that provides the necessary structure(s) and support, and joins with the other resources of the community, including educators, mental health practitioners, and community-based services and programs, the "therapeutic" potential of the school for both individual students of concern, and for all students, will be significant. Schools that have these components contribute to the building and maintaining of "resiliency" and self-esteem for those who are referred for mental health assistance as well as all of the other students in the school.

We have always believed the purpose of mental health work and education to be essentially the same; that being to nurture the positive developmental thrust of childhood and adolescence, and to help in overcoming any stumbling blocks to its progression.

References

1   DeWitt, Peter, and Slade, Sean, *School Climate Change: How to Build a Positive Environment for Learning*, Alexandria, Virginia, Association for Curriculum and Supervision Development, 2014.

2   School for Integrated Academics and Technologies, Los Angeles Unified School District, n.d.

3   Gonzales, Luis D., *School Climate: 180 Degree Turn, Negative to Positive*, Los Angeles, CA, Los Angeles County Office of Education, Division of Evaluation, Attendance and Pupil Services, n.d.

Case Management

A Creative Philosophy and Form of Practice

As has already been described in a number of places in the manual, it is true that those interventions/actions decided in good faith at the Care Team, an SST, or the SART conference, are only as good as the follow-up that ensures implementation of the strategies agreed at the meeting. Nevertheless, many people confuse follow-up with "case management". In fact, the seven-step case management process starts much before the follow-up responsibilities. Let's take a closer look.

The Problem that Case Management Seeks to Address

The problems of our current service delivery system include services that are crisis oriented and lack an emphasis on prevention, services that divide the problems of children and families into distinct categories that fail to reflect interrelated causes and solutions, a lack of collaboration and communication among the various public and private agencies, and the inability of specialized agencies to easily craft comprehensive solutions to complex problems. There is also a need to improve the coordination and integration of efforts within the school and school system, and those can also be factors that contribute to dysfunction.

Is the term "Case Management" a User-friendly Term?

Although the term case management is used in a variety of settings by professionals from various disciplines, and sometimes by untrained personnel who hook on to this much too often used term, it is not a term that truly reflects either the philosophy or this form of practice. To some "case management" implies that those who carry the term of

DOI: 10.4324/9781003240266-9

case manager are controlling or "managing" their clients, and doing the work for them. We must be careful not to use this term with our students and their parents/guardians, as it can certainly be off putting and sound derogatory. If someone were to say to a student or parent/guardian "I am your case manager", the client may be well within their rights to say, "I am not a case and I do not need to be managed", and who could blame them for that kind of retort? In reality, what is called case management is actually an empowerment philosophy and form of practice, where the care/case manager works in collaboration with the student/family to develop and implement a package of services that best addresses their needs.

Some terms that may be more appropriate than case management are: Care coordination, student/family centered comprehensive services development and implementation, and service coordination. Because the term case management is so commonly used, it will be utilized in this Chapter as well. Remember not to use this term with your students and caregivers because of the negative connotation that it implies.

The Importance of the Relationship

The case management process is dependent on the unique relationship between the student/family and the care, or case manager. This relationship is the heart of the process. This is a relationship built on trust, and the importance of that relationship cannot be overstated. The care/case manager metaphorically provides the "glue" that helps to keep the plan together, and provides continuity over time, one that is necessary to bring about the agreed upon goals and changes. However, this is only done after the first steps in the process have been accomplished.

Why Schools?

Schools remain the one institution of society that are on the frontline. All of the problems and issues of the society are visible in the schools because children bring these issues with them when they enter the schoolhouse door. Our schools are the magnifying glasses of our society. We, who work in and with schools, find ourselves in a unique position to develop, implement and monitor those comprehensive plans tailored to address a student's needs. Schools are the natural place where children's needs and resources can be joined.

Although case management was not initially a function of education, we know that a child's education can be enhanced by addressing the social, health, psychological and other issues are affecting their ability to progress. Therefore, it is important that a member of Care Team, the Student Success Team, or the School Attendance Review Team, be s/he a school social worker, a counselor, a nurse, or another member of the team, assumes the role of care/case manager, whether they are called by that name or not.

Case Management: A Definition for Schools

Case management is a method of providing services, whereby the case manager, in collaboration with other members of the student support team(s), along with the student and his or her family, determines appropriate strategies and actions to address the needs of a student. When appropriate, the case manager arranges, provides, advocates for, coordinates, monitors, and evaluates the overall implementation of the plan. The goal is to develop and implement a package of services that are comprehensive, culturally appropriate, and delivered in a caring way.

The term "management" refers to the improved coordination and connectedness of services and resources that our students receive because of the efforts on their behalf by the case manager who works in collaboration with the student and family. While all of the words encompassed in this definition are important, coordination and connectedness are probably the key ones. If the plan for the student/family is not coordinated, and if the connections stated in the service/action plan do not happen, the plan will most likely fail.

The Case Manager: A Definition

The case manager is the primary person who, through the personal relationship with the student and his or her family, provides the foundation for motivation and support in providing, coordinating, advocating for, and maintaining the network of services and resources necessary to maintain academic and social progress. The case manager works with the student and caregivers to define and develop a package of services that are comprehensive, flexible, client-centered, coordinated, goal oriented, and therefore, more effective.

The goal of the case manager is to empower each of the participants of the plan to follow through on the responsibilities they assumed in the service/action planning phase, and to do so in a timely manner. The case manager's work is to ensure that the plan takes effect. The case manager is always working to empower the client to do as much for himself/herself as possible, but is flexible enough to "pick up the ball" when that seems necessary. The case manager does not want to do too much or too little, and walks a sort of tightrope in making sure that the package of services actually comes together. The case manager has to tread a fine line regarding when or whether he or she takes a more active role in working to ensure that the action items are put into place. At times this requires encouragement, advocacy, and/or monitoring, or in some instances, "taking the bull by the horns" to "glue" together the various action items.

Keep in mind that the case manager is the "primary provider" of the service plan. Other programs and resources are mobilized when there are things that the case manager cannot do by himself or herself.

89

The Steps in the Case Management Process

1. **Identification and Outreach**

   Often those who are most in need of support do not seek our services on their own, or do not know how to go about getting them. Often, access is not user-friendly, or the motivation is not sufficient to get through the "hoops" necessary to obtain the needed services. Students show their needs in the school setting, either through their grades, poor attendance, visits to the school nurse with unidentified complaints, disciplinary and behavioral problems, revealing papers written and turned in to teachers, and, at times, a direct request to a staff member. If we pay attention to these warning signs, we can easily identify those students who might benefit from case management services and, by extension, their families. These young people might not be asking for services, but are nevertheless the perfect ones to receive case management services.

2. **Engagement**

   This is a most crucial step in the process. If a relationship of trust is not developed between the care/case manager and student, along with his/her family, there is very little chance that any service plan will be successful. There is no set number of meetings that are required, but the case manager must give the student/family a sense that their interest in them is genuine, and that they have the intention to stick with them for a significant period of time. As previously stated, this relationship will serve as the basis for the motivation to keep the plan alive, and to make sure that it is implemented. The case manager must impart to the student/family that they are a person of integrity, and will follow-through with their end of the responsibilities.

3. **Intake and Assessment**

   Although the case manager will most likely be collecting information about the student/family and their situation prior to this step, Intake and Assessment is a more formalized process of uncovering the areas that are the stressors and barriers to success. Once the trusting relationship has been established, the student/family will be much more open to questions that are more intrusive into their personal lives. Questions such as the living situation/housing, income and employment, likes and dislikes about school, learning issues, peer relationships, alcohol, tobacco and drug use/abuse, general health and wellness, sexuality, nutrition, and goals/hopes for their future.

4. **Development of the Service/Care Plan**

   Until the case manager has a good idea of the issues, their possible interrelationships and origins, s/he will be unable to collaboratively develop a service plan of action in partnership with the student/family. Once the case manager has a good sense of the areas to be addressed, s/he works in partnership with the student/family to define the plan that will be put into action. We cannot emphasize enough the importance of collaboratively developing the plan; we do that "with them", not "to them", as has been repeated a number of times in this book. This is consistent with the philosophy of case management as an empowerment model of practice. The more the student can define their own goals and the places where they see issues they need to address, the better, and the less to do for the case manager.

When one has no stake in the way things are, when one's needs or opinions are provided no forum, when one sees oneself as the object of unilateral actions, it takes no particular wisdom to suggest that one would rather be elsewhere.

[1]

Many schools and agencies use a chart and forms that define the goal, the service(s) that are needed, the "who" and the "when" a particular service will be implemented. Many also define "benchmarks" along the way to measure progress. The school or district might have such "tools" for student support staff to use uniformly.

5. **Implementation of the Plan, Including Linkages to Needed Services**

With close attention to the "who" and the "when", efforts to implement the plan get started. Yes, this might seem like a long way from step 1, but again, this is a process that follows defined steps. As has already been said, it is important that the responsibilities are shared and no one person, the student, teacher, staff member or family member, be burdened with too much of the responsibility. When there is shared responsibility, a sense of teamwork is established and individuals feel some responsibility to bring others along with their own responsibilities. The case manager will also undertake some responsibilities that s/he are best able to perform and/or implement. By undertaking some of the responsibilities for the actions to be implemented, the case manager imparts that s/he is a member of the team.

6. **Monitoring and Modification, When Needed**

It is very important to monitor the benchmarks and other indicators that the service plan has been put into effect. It is also important to obtain feedback from the student/family on how things are going, and whether the opportunities, services and supports are working. At times it is necessary to modify the service/care plan for one reason or another. Therefore, the case manager needs to maintain regular communication with the student/family, and a willingness to help in whatever way is necessary to bring about success.

7. **Evaluation**

It goes without saying that evaluation is more important today than ever. Every funding source wants to see outcome data. When serving humans, qualitative data are just as important as quantitative data. Therefore, changes that are perceived by the student him/herself, teachers, family members and others are just as important as those things that can be measured.

Once Again, the "Broad Range of Interventions"

When developing a service plan from the base of the school, the case worker should consider a number of areas for intervention, often referred to as a "broad range of interventions".

Classroom

Many students will have academic difficulties which can take a number of forms. Poor grades, lack of mastery with a certain subject(s), or a poor connection with the teacher. The classroom teacher(s) are very significant in any service plan involving the classroom, and its potential success. Teacher training does not always include classroom academic and behavior strategies. Working collaboratively with the teacher on behalf of the student can be of great significance. It should be no surprise that, of the millions of students referred for Special Education assessment each year, the majority are for the suspicion of a Learning Disability, one of the twelve "disabling" conditions included in the Federal Special Education law. Many believe that a large number of these students could be helped by classroom interventions if the team were to take the time to find strategies that would address the issue. With regard to classroom interventions, if these are part of the service/care plan/contract, it might be a good idea for the case manager to be the one who assumes this responsibility as s/he will most likely be the best one to work with the teacher(s) on behalf of the student. Once again, a good service/care plan should contain enough interventions for the responsibilities to be shared by various members of the team.

The Larger School Environment

To the extent that the school has developed various opportunities, services and supports within or beyond the school environment, in the school district or the larger community, team members and the case manager have resources from which to choose as part of the action plan. The case manager needs to be familiar with such details as who the contact person is, any special eligibility requirements, the time, place and duration of the service or program referred to. The student should be encouraged to seek out this information for her/himself, but the case manager should be ready to fill in any details that were missed by the student.

As stated in a previous chapter, the climate and culture of the school itself can be a therapeutic tool for children and youth. If the student is in some formal therapy, either within or outside of the school, the therapeutic work can be reinforced, or have a counter therapeutic effect in the daily experiences by the student in the environment of the school. The positive relations that are developed between staff members and the student, the range of choices made available to the student to develop interests and skills in art, music, and athletics, can all go a long way in developing or reinforcing self-esteem.

The case manager should check with the student after a reasonable period of time to see whether the student has made the connection to the campus program or service recommended. Here again, the relationship is key in using encouragement and advocacy to "glue" together student needs with services.

In/With the Home

The stressors within the family can be part of the problem, and the strengths of the family can be part of the solution. Stressors might include housing, the development of employment related skills, health care, respite, food and clothing deficiencies, and the need for more education. Strengths include those things that the parents/guardians can do to support the student's learning. Regular communication with the school, requiring daily or weekly progress reports, arranging for a time and place to do homework and reading, taking the student for a medical exam, participation in family therapy, obtaining a needed service or program for their youth, spending more quality time with the student, and implementing rewards and consequences. Joining with the family can and is very important in the development and implementation of a care/service plan/contract. The worker might encounter a good deal of resistance from the family, and the worker will have to spend time trying to understand these resistances and help to overcome them. Here again, the importance of the relationship cannot be overstated. The trust level that will lead to a true partnership takes time, and will only come when the family sees that the case manager has the best interest of their child as his/her primary goal. The family should be reminded how the teamwork effort that everyone is working on together can have a profoundly positive impact on their child/student. Steps toward positive changes can and do occur.

Checking in at respectful intervals can serve as a prompt to the family. These check-ins can also be used to provide updates on how other aspects of the plan are going, and the latest progress of their youngster at school. Families frequently complain that the school did not keep them informed of how things have been going, and this interval check-in creates that opportunity as well. The case manager will have to decide whether the check-in should be face-to-face contact or over the phone. Face-to-face is thought to be better, especially when more complex issues of resistance are to be discussed. Of course, scheduling and time constraints are always a consideration.

In the Community

It is important that the case manager should have a good understanding of the range of services, the agencies, providers and programs of the community. Most communities have service directories provided by the United Way or another reputable umbrella organization. Today, many of these are available on the internet. Schools can easily purchase or obtain access to these directories as another resource for the Care Team, SST or the SART at the school. One of the most effective ways to ensure a referral to a particular agency or provider is to supply the name and contact information to the student/caregiver(s) with whom the care/case manager has a personal connection. This can be much more effective than just to give them the name and phone number of an agency. Here again, these personal relationships have a significant place in case management practice.

93

As stated in a previous Chapter, another suggestion for effecting a referral to a community agency or provider is to use the school setting for the first meeting between the two parties. This can serve to "bridge" the referral, and create a better chance that it will actually happen. We all have hesitancies about approaching the unknown, and a face-to-face meeting at the school between agency representatives along with the student and family may well serve the actual follow-through.

Core Principles of Case Management

1. **Case management requires partnership**
    Case management is first and foremost a system of partnerships, between the case/care manager and the student, his or her family, and between organizations. In an effective case management system, the case manager works in partnership "with" the student/family, and shares responsibilities with them, rather than working "on" them.

2. **Case management communicates respect for the student and family**
    The success of any case management effort depends on the degree to which the young person is engaged in the development and joint ownership of the service/care plan contract, and has a major stake in ensuring its success. In every aspect, the student has to be treated as a mature, responsible person, not a number or a child.

3. **Case management must provide predictability**
    Many disadvantaged students experience their life as a series of random events over which they have little or no control. Successful case/care management works to rebuild that sense of control and predictability by helping young people to plan, to set goals, and to undertake a process of meeting those goals. Young people learn that they can make choices, and that their actions lead directly to concrete outcomes for them.

Qualifications for Case Managers

1. **Disciplined Empathy**
    Effective case managers seem to exhibit what might be called "disciplined empathy". They respect and care about their clients, and can develop partnerships with those clients. They listen to what clients say, read between the lines, and size them up. They can work with the student/family to mutually develop a service/care plan that can be "owned" by both the student/family and the case/care manager. Case/care managers have a compassionate but tough-minded understanding of the youth they work with, an aptitude to develop an alliance with them, as well as the ability to challenge and confront youth to meet their responsibilities, when needed.

2. **Partnership Skills**

   At the same time, case managers have to have the skills to develop partnerships with institutions. Diplomatic sensitivity is a key trait. Case managers negotiate with bureaucracies for services. To do so requires adept social skills and an ability to understand institutional cultures. Case/care managers need to adopt a philosophy that barriers to client self-determination are both internal and external, and constantly interact. Interventions must often aim at changing both the individual and the environment.

3. **Empowerment**

   Case/Care managers need the ability to help students/families develop and effectively utilize their own internal problem solving and coping resources.

Case (Care) Management: Key Concepts

1. Service or care coordination is a more user-friendly term for the practice often called "case management".

2. Our schools are in a unique position to address the needs of the "whole child" and his/her family. Our schools are the great magnifying glasses of society. The students bring their issues with them to school on a daily basis, and these are often visible in the school setting.

3. The trusting relationship between the case manager, the student, and his or her family, is the heart of the process.

4. The trust that builds between the client(s) and care/care manager sustains the partnership toward shared goals.

5. The case management relationship empowers the student and family by joining with them in a plan of success, and serves as the foundation for motivation and support.

6. We convey the belief to our students/clients that they have the power to improve their situations.

7. The ownership of the service/care plan by the student/family is a significant factor in whether the efforts/interventions planned will be effective.

8. The importance of the care/case manager to empower the student/family and, when appropriate, the willingness of the care/case manager to take a more active role to ensure the service/care/contract items are put into place. It is like walking a tightrope, not doing too much or too little, always adjusting the balance based on the circumstances.

9. Familiarity by the case/care manager with the range of intervention resources that can be utilized in the classroom, the larger school environment, in/with the home, and the larger community.

10. Developing personal relationships with service providers can help to bridge clients to services that are not provided directly by the care/case manager.

11. The coordination and connectedness that occurs due to the efforts of the student/client(s) and care/case manager, as they work together to implement a plan of success.

12. Checking in at respectful intervals is very important.

Reference

1 Sarason, Seymour, *The Predictable Failure of Educational Reform: Can We Change Before it is Too Late?*, San Francisco, Jossey-Bass, 1993.

10 | Making the Home-School Connection a Positive One

Before connecting with families, care must be taken to ensure that the connection with parents/guardians will be the most positive experience possible. SST and SART coordinators/facilitators do not want to add to a history of bad experiences that parents or guardians might have had with schools, nor do they want to start off on the wrong foot. Almost all teachers and administrators want to involve families in schools, but many have not been trained or prepared to build positive and productive partnerships with families from diverse cultures, backgrounds and ethnicities. Here are things to keep in mind in helping to make a positive connection possible.

* Research is in universal agreement that family involvement in the child's education is directly linked to student achievement, positive attendance, and a stronger connection with the school.
* The communication style of the school or staff, and the communication style of the family might not match. In this context, "communication" style is not limited to language only, but is also based on our own lived experiences, lifestyle choices, or awareness of ethnic differences, and all of these can affect positive communication free of any conscious or unconscious bias. School staff need to be sensitive to this possibility.
* Family members' experiences when they were in school, and their prior experiences in their child's school affects how open and trusting they are with school requests for their participation. Negative experiences have a cumulative effect and can become barriers to building a strong collaborative relationship between the school and the family.
* Years of hearing negative comments about their youth, and documentation of behavioral issues, or "school failure", can have a toxic effect on the relationship between school and home, and upon the expectations that family members have of a student.

DOI: 10.4324/9781003240266-10

* Many families are involved and invested in their children's education, but tell researchers that they must feel Trust before agreeing to attend or participate in events at school. Trust may take time and experience to build, and staff might experience hesitancy on the part of the family at first.

Parent Communication and Involvement Tip Sheet

1. A sign that says "Parents and Visitors are Welcome" should be posted on the front door of the school.
2. Designate or hire a parent liaison or family-school coordinator who is a participant on the School Coordinated Care Team (SCCT), Student Success Team (SST) process, and/or the Student Attendance Review Team (SART).
3. Create a parent/teacher outreach team whose focus is on parent involvement.
4. There should be evidence of celebrating diversity of the student body on bulletin boards and activities.
5. Parents and guardians want to know that their children are being challenged academically in a caring, safe and supportive environment.
6. A parent room or center can be established that will offer workshops/discussion groups for/with families on school-related matters, as well as parenting challenges and issues, and can be a positive addition to any school.
7. Encourage parents and community members to share their skills, careers and interests with students, as part of classroom activities and presentations.
8. Parents/guardians want to know that their children are being challenged academically in a caring, safe and supportive environment.
9. Make the school building available to parents and community residents for educational, recreational, and social activities.
10. Create a regular school-family newsletter that lists opportunities for parents/guardians to become involved in leadership roles in the school, as well as other opportunities for them to increase their participation.
11. Provide handouts for parents/guardians regarding how they can become involved in the school, supporting education in the home, and tips for navigating the school and school district.
12. Unfortunately, some parents only receive communication from the school regarding disruptive behavior or lack of academic achievement. Instead, communicate something positive about the child's social behavior or academic achievement and/or the child's strengths. Good news can reinforce itself both for the student and their family.
13. Invite parents to school to participate in a positive experience such as a special art activity or a student drama production. If their children are involved or participating, there is a much better chance they will attend.

14. The addition of a "pot luck" as part of the event can be a real incentive for attending.

15. Regularly assess family involvement efforts using questionnaires, telephone interviews, meetings, and discussion groups, to learn which parent involvement issues have the best chance for success.

16. Provide information and opportunities to parents/caregivers whose first language is not English. Make sure that the program involves staff members and school volunteers from diverse backgrounds to help families feel comfortable to ask questions.

17. Some schools are creating "Welcome Centers" where immigrant families are assisted with information about citizenship classes, accessing medical and dental services, food pantries, and other needed supports. In many cities, community colleges are offering English as a Second Language (ESL) programs in local schools.

18. Sending out calendars with lunch menus, along with a listing of other important meetings, classes along with various opportunities to volunteer.

19. Offer drop-in "child watch" when parents/guardians come to school for an event.

20. Invite parents/guardians to serve on planning committees, such as the School Site Council, steering committees, as well as district level councils and committees.

21. Conferences with every parent or guardian at least once a year, with follow-ups as needed.

22. Offer fun activities for the whole family, such as barbecues, beach days, camp outs.

23. Provide in-service for teachers and staff regarding culturally proficient meetings with parents and guardians, such as in parent/teacher conferences.

24. Communication examples:
    * Use technology to enhance communication via computer or text to share information about the school, and for sharing attendance patterns, homework assignments, and other useful information regarding students.
    * Home visits by the teacher, principal, parent liaison, and other student support staff can be very useful.
    * Enhance the quality of communication by translating letters and written materials into the primary language of the home, and providing interpreters at parent meetings.
    * Provide weekly or monthly folders of student work that are sent home and reviewed by the caregivers, added their comments and returned to the school.
    * Provide in-service and tips to teachers and other school staff on positive parent/guardian communication practices.

Examples of Unwelcoming School Experiences for Parents/Guardians

* Being ignored by school personnel when they arrive at the school.
* Arriving for a scheduled appointment and made to wait more than an hour.

* Being told "you should have called first" when they drop by.
* Being asked to "sign in" before a pleasant greeting such as "Hello, how can I help you?".
* Being told they may not go to their child's classroom without a scheduled appointment.
* When educators recognize the importance of parents and guardians being involved at school, but struggle to develop sustainable plans for meaningful engagement, particularly among families of color and recent immigrants.
* When some families who are less visibly involved in their children's school are perceived in a somewhat negative manner when they do come to school and want their voice to be heard. The lack of visibility on the part of the family can be interpreted as indifference, lack of concern, or different values. Research and direct inquiry show this is not the case. There must be appreciation that families are often dealing with real barriers to greater involvement, such as work hours, incarceration and illness.

Parents/Guardians Feel Welcome to the School When

* When they are greeted in a friendly manner.
* When verbal and non-verbal communication is approachable.
* When staff members slow down and take time to repeat information when needed.
* When parent(s)/guardian(s) are addressed by their last name in a respectful tone.
* When people introduce them to nearby school personnel.
* When they feel that school personnel genuinely have their child's best interest at heart.
* When school personnel reach out to them through telephone calls, text messages, email and handwritten notes.
* When the school provides opportunities for parents/guardians to connect with others.
* When families from diverse cultures are welcomed and represented.
* When parent feedback and suggestions are honored and respected.

Some Possible Roles for Parents/Guardians in Schools

* Serve as teacher aides.
* Aides in Special Education resource rooms.
* Providing information on various services/resources to other parents/guardians.

* Developing parent support groups.
* Serving as health aides.
* Assist with attendance outreach.
* Tutoring.
* Homework clubs.
* Cafeteria support during lunch.
* Before and after school programs, developing evening and weekend recreation and playground activities.
* Offering cultural programs that feature the diverse cultures in the school.
* Developing ethnic heritage educational programs.
* Multi-lingual assistance.
* Running a parent library.
* Staffing a parent resource center.
* Arts and theater assistance.
* Developing micro enterprises such as child watch.
* Promoting job clubs and obtaining classroom speakers.
* Helping to plan family fun nights.
* Developing a school store.
* Developing a clothing bank.
* Developing barter programs among parents/guardians.
* Doing community needs and assets assessments.
* Serving as hallway monitors and in safety programs.
* Addressing lice issues.
* Developing a "big buddy" program.
* Participating in the development of classes and workshops for parents/guardians on special issues such as health care, parent child conflict, control and violence issues, parenting classes, and how to start a small business.

11 | Positive Behavioral Support vs. the Punishment Paradigm

In the overall culture and climate of a school, there are consequences needed in response to behavioral or attitudinal issues exhibited by some students. It is very important that the consequences be fair and equitably enforced, that the consequence(s) are calculated and tempered with the extent of the misbehavior, whenever possible. If the consequences of a behavioral issue can be a teaching/learning opportunity for the student, that would be great (i.e., rather than being suspended for smoking, have the student do research from the American Lung Association and write a paper on what they found). Punitive interventions do not motivate a student to change, to believe that he or she is capable of achieving success, or to learn resiliency skills. Yet, for too much of the time, our schools resort to negative measures to effect behavioral change. Thirteen states still allow corporal punishment to be inflicted by school personnel. These practices are not working very well.

Certainly, if a student commits a violent crime, sells drugs, assaults a teacher, or brings a weapon to school, to name a few, these can lead to expulsion from the school district, and most likely will lead to consequences by the police and the courts. These are a small minority of offenses that occur at or around the school. The majority of offenses that qualify for suspension are discretionary, and reasonable alternatives are permissible. If the school can develop a listing of alternatives to suspension for those offenses that can lead to suspension, this can be very useful to keeping students engaged in/with the school.

Some of the concerns with the punishment paradigm are discussed below:

The Punishment Paradigm:

* Reinforces Negative Attention-Seeking Patterns:
  Students with serious behavioral concerns have learned that the surest way to gain attention is to act out. These students are used to being punished, and this treatment becomes a way of life. Such students might not be happy with the results of

DOI: 10.4324/9781003240266-11

this pattern of behavior, but there is a sense of safety and familiarity in this routine that they know and understand. Such behavior can give them a sense of control because they know the outcome of the behavior.

* Confirms the Student's Own Poor Self-Concept:
Students who have a pattern of misbehavior usually have a low self-concept. They know they are "bad" and they expect to be punished. This expectation can become a self-fulfilling prophecy since the student expects to be punished because he or she is "no good". Such students may not believe they have any other choice.

* Rewards Non-Compliance Through Peer Status:
Some students learn to seek status with their friends through being disrespectful toward authority figures. These students can become leaders in the eyes of their peers as they prove how tough they are by acting out, and then enduring or evading the punishment. Often, other students will follow a negative leader. The more this leader acts out and is punished, the more he or she feels powerful, and the more status is gained with his or her peers.

* May Increase Student Resistance and Set Up Power Struggles:
Punishment does not build healthy relationships. A head on collision between the person in authority and the student usually produces a wreck. Punishment can give the person in authority a feeling of power, but it might destroy the relationship, that one significant relationship that could have made a difference.

* Does Not Address the Roots of the Concern:
Punishment does not address the reason for the misbehavior. Until the underlying reason for the misbehavior is understood, such a response only complicates the situation and might not solve anything at all. The negative behavior is serving the student in some way, or he or she would not be doing it. Until the reason for the behavior is uncovered and addressed, little progress will be accomplished.

* Does Not Teach Appropriate Behavior:
Punishing negative behavior may temporarily stop the behavior, but it does not teach better behavior. Students need to learn how to make positive, useful and informed behavioral choices to achieve the success they deserve. Rather than punishing students, their teachers and parents need to be able to teach them how to make these positive and pro-social choices.

School staff who rely on negative and punitive disciplinary measures will not produce student success. Teams need to help students to build healthy self-concepts and teach (and model) students to make good choices for success. Interventions must be designed to build on student positive strengths, rather than to punish them.

However, part of learning is that all choices have consequences, good and bad. Consequences are a part of real life. If students break the rules, they need to learn to accept responsibility for the consequences of their behavior. Schools must have clear and consistent rules, and enforce them in an equitable and consistent way. These clear and consistent boundaries can give students a sense of safety and security. Students with a pattern of misbehavior need to learn what their strengths are, and how to use them effectively to build success for themselves.

Principals and other school administrators are increasingly seeking ways to address behaviors with non-punitive measures. Effective student support teams may encounter adult (staff) behaviors that can have the effect of exacerbating student learning and behavioral difficulties. Providing in-service training and workshops on effective classroom management strategies, and the positive effects of developing personal relationships with students, can go a long way to minimizing the contributions of adults to what is manifested in the students.

The Hurt that Troubled Children Create is Never Greater than the Hurt that they Feel

While there is a variety of causes for students' behavioral manifestations, all of them draw attention to the self.

What is the student really saying by this behavior?

* Look at me, talk to me, be with me.
* I'm unhappy.
* I'm mad.
* I'm sad.
* I'm frustrated.
* I'm tired.
* I need something.
* I want something, or maybe I need something.
* I'm hungry.

Some of the things the student may need are:

* Attention.
* Reinforcement.
* Rules that are clear, purposeful, consistent and caringly enforced.
* Logical consequences for misbehavior.
* Regular monitoring.
* Acknowledgement.
* A sense of mastery.
* Limits.

* A reward.
* Feedback from those who are affected by this behavior.
* Modeling.
* A feeling of comfort.
* Opportunities for growth and the accompanying increase in responsibility.
* Relaxation.
* Food.
* Unconditional love.

List of Appendices

Sample forms and materials from various school districts
The forms that appear in the book, along with additional forms and documents, can be downloaded from www.routledge.com/9781032146294.

Appendix 1: School Coordinated Care Team (SCCT)

1. Figure A.1. School Coordinated Care Team Sample Flow Chart
   Example of a Flow Chart

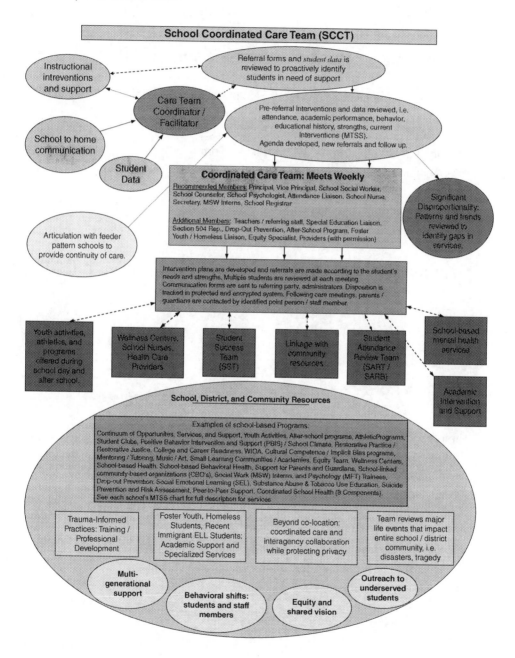

2. Teacher Input Form, Dorchester USD
3. SCCT Sample Agenda
4. Confidentiality Agreement
5. School Coordinated Services Plan document, Mt. Diablo Unified School District (MDUSD)

Appendix 2: Student Success Team (SST)

1. Request for Assistance/SST Form, San Francisco Unified School District (SFUSD)
2. Student Success Team Parent/Guardian Brochure (2 pages)
3. SST Summary Form
4. Example of a Seriously Limited SST Summary Form
5. Example of an Exemplary SST Summary Form
6. SST Follow-Up Form
7. Example of a Seriously Limited SST Follow-Up Form

Appendix 3: Student Attendance Review Team (SART)

1. Example of a SART Contract, BUSD

The following documents can be downloaded from www.routledge.com/9781032146294:

Student Success Team

1. Parent Guardian Invite to an SST
2. Sample SST Action Plan (Vertical Format), SFUSD
3. Sample SST Follow-Up Form (Vertical Format) SFUSD
4. Developmental/Family History Form, SFUSD (2 pages)
5. Observation of the Learning Environment Form
6. Supplemental Request for an SST for an English Language Learner
7. Parent/Guardian Invitation to an SST Meeting, Spanish
8. SST Parent/Guardian Brochure, Spanish (2 pages)
9. Developmental/Family History, Spanish (2 pages)
10. SST Summary Form, Spanish
11. SST Follow-up Form, Spanish
12. Family/Developmental History, Chinese (2 pages)
13. SST Summary Form, Chinese

14. SST Follow-up Form, Chinese
15. SST Summary Form, Vietnamese
16. SST Follow-Up Form, Vietnamese
17. Stages of SST Development (2 pages)
18. SST Log Form

Appendix 1

School Coordinated Care Team
(SCCT) Appendix

Dorchester County Public Schools
Student Success Team (SST)
Teacher Input Form – Secondary

To (Teacher):_____   Date:_____

Re: (Student)_____   From:_____

1. **Key Questions:**

Check appropriate description:	Always	Usually	Sometimes	Never
Attends class				
Is on time				
Comes to class prepared				
Completes class assignments				
Turns in homework				
Follows directions independently				
Needs help to complete tasks				

2. Grades are: Improving_____   Holding_____   Slipping_____

3. Current grade is: A_____   B_____   C_____   D_____   E_____

4. Behavior: Excellent_____ Satisfactory_____ Inconsistent_____ Unsatisfactory_____

5. **Strengths:**
_____
_____
_____
_____

6. **Areas of Concern:**
_____
_____
_____
_____

7. **Additional Comments/Recommendation for the Team:**
_____
_____
_____
_____

Signature:_____

Thank you for your valuable feedback and cooperation!

School Coordinated Care Team (SCCT) Agenda

School: _____

Date: _____

A. New Students:

    1. _____ 2. _____

    2. _____ 4. _____

    5. _____ 6. _____

B. Follow-up Students:

    1. _____ 2. _____

    3. _____ 4. _____

    5. _____ 6. _____

    7. _____ 8. _____

C. SST's Scheduled: Location   Date   Time

    1. _____ _____ _____ _____

    2. _____ _____ _____ _____

    3. _____ _____ _____ _____

    4. _____ _____ _____ _____

    5. _____ _____ _____ _____

D. Program/Service Need/Coordination Issues:

    1. _____

    2. _____

    3. _____

E. Agenda Items for next meeting:

    1. _____ 2. _____

_____School

Coordinated Care Team

Confidentiality Agreement

Program Staff and Extended Team Members

I, the undersigned, hereby agree not to divulge any information or records concerning any name of students, family members, or other individuals of the _____school District community, without proper authorization in accordance with the state and federal law and interagency agreements. I recognize that any discussion of or release of information to any unauthorized person is forbidden and may be grounds for legal and/or other disciplinary action.

During the performance of my assigned duties, I will have access to confidential information required for effective service coordination and delivery. I agree that all discussions, records, and information generated or maintained in connection with these activities will not be disclosed to any unauthorized person.

Confidentiality Agreement:

1. I will comply with confidentiality law and policy as it pertains to securing, orally, sharing, copying or recording confidential information and records of any individuals and families about whom I obtain information.

2. I will restrict requests for access to _____(name of district) and other agencies confidential information and records; and limit sharing of confidential information to those authorized to formulate and implement a case specific service plan as specified in WIC 1989.40 and WIC 1898.45. (CA law)

I recognize that the unauthorized release of confidential information may expose me to civil/criminal liability and a penalty of $10,000, court costs, and reasonable attorney fees.

Signature: _____date:_____

Print name: _____Job Title: _____

Received by: _____
        Signature of authorized personnel

Staff Name:

Date:

Mt. Diablo Unified School District
School Linked Services
Student Coordinated Services Plan

CONFIDENTIAL

Student Name:

Parent/Guardian Name(s) / Address:

Grade: _____ School: _____

Tel #
Cell#'s

Student Cell Phone:

☐ Foster Youth   Social Worker (Child Welfare): _____
☐ Juvenile Probation   Probation Officer: _____
☐ HOPE (McKinney Vento / Homeless) ☐ Unaccompanied Minor
☐ Group Home Supervisor:

Language Spoken at Home:

☐ Special Education ☐ Sec. 504

Ethnicity:

Gender:

Date of last IEP?
IEP Case Manager:

Student/Counselor Collaborative Goals (self-determination):

1)

2)

3)

1. **Parent/ Caregiver Contact**
   ☐ Phone Call (Date): _____   ☐ Meeting (Date): _____
2. **School Based Collaborative Meeting**
   ☐ Care Team ☐ SST ☐ IEP ☐ 504 ☐ PBT ☐ Other: _____
3. **Transitional Meetings**
   ☐ End of Service (date) _____ ☐ End of Service (TAY) (date) _____ ☐ YTM (FYS) (date) _____
   (Meetings above (1, 2,3) are requisite for ALL students receiving services)

Notes:

114

Date	Action Plan	Target Date	Notes
	Student will: 1) 2) 3)		
	Parent / Guardian will: 1) 2) 3)		
	School Social Worker / Staff will: 1) 2) 3)		
	Other person will:		
	Other person will:		

Possible barriers to achieving goals and plans to address them:

OTHER AGENCIES / SUPPORT TEAM / PEOPLE SUPPORTING STUDENT TO REACH THEIR GOALS

Name	Agency / Role / Relationship	Tel # / Email	Role / Notes

Interagency Collaboration / Plan for Coordinated and Integrated Services:

Benchmarks:

Parent / Guardian Signature _____ Date _____

Student Signature _____ Date _____

Staff Signature _____ Date _____

Participant Signature _____ Date _____

Appendix 2

Student Success Team (SST)
Appendix

SAN FRANCISCO UNIFIED SCHOOL DISTRICT
Wellness/Student Assistance Program/Student Success Team
Request for Assistance (1.0)*
Wellness/SAP/SST

Referring Person	Class/Period	School	Grade	Date

Student	HO#	D. O.B.	Gender	Ethnicity

Parent/Caregiver	Phone Number	Student's Primary Language/Language of Home	Language Proficiency

1. Student's Strengths Noted

❑ Regular attendance	❑ Follows instructions
❑ Cooperative with others	❑ Participates in class
❑ Able to problem solve	❑ Sets goals
❑ Makes/maintains friendships	❑ Helpful to others
❑ Negotiates/compromises	❑ Communicates needs
❑ Articulates feelings	❑ Asks for help
❑ Good Listener	❑ Sense of humor
❑ Other:	❑ Attentive in class

2. Reason for Request

- ❑ Academic
- ❑ Attendance
- ❑ Behavioral/Attitude
- ❑ Health Issues
- ❑ Family Concerns
- ❑ Other:

3. Interventions/Modifications/Adaptations (Please describe in comments section below. Include length of time these have been tried):

❑ Instructional modifications	❑ Tutoring	❑ Caregiver conference
❑ Classroom modifications	❑ After-school program	❑ Detention
❑ Other:		

COMMENTS: _____

*********************** (Referral Source - Complete To This Point) ***********************

4. Student Profile Section (Counselor/SAP/SST Team to complete):

STAR 9 (Two previous yrs): Year	Reading	Lang	Math	District & Community-based services currently (c) or previously (p) received:
				GATE English Plus ELD/ELL Tutoring Special Education Grade(s) Repeated
				Mental Health Mentoring Peer Resource Other
Date of Vision Screening:	Results:		Date of Hearing Screening:	Results:

5. Date of discussion with family regarding concerns, and explanation of the SAP/SST/Wellness process: _____
Results: _____

***********************Feedback To Referring Person***********************

❑ SAP/SST date:	❑ Referral to tutoring	❑ Met with caregiver, date:
❑ Referred to support services	❑ Met with student, date:	❑ Referred to After-school program
❑ Other:		

COMMENTS:_____

Wellness/SAP/SST/ Team Member	Date

* When making referrals, please utilize cumulative folder, copy and attach student locator card, current report card, and the 2.1 Teacher Input Form from each teacher. Careful consideration should be given to the impact of language, culture, health, and environmental factors in planning appropriate interventions, modifications, and adaptations.

Wellness/SAP/SST 1.0

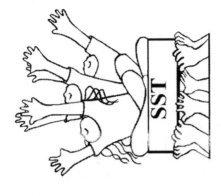

STUDENT SUCCESS TEAM

SST

Parents · School · Community

Parent Brochure

(Name & address of School)

What is the Future?

At the end of the meeting, a follow up date will be scheduled to review progress. You will be invited to meet again with members of the SST to evaluate changes and growth in your student.

Additional testing through Special Education resources may be recommended at this time. This recommendation comes from the members of the SST only after modifications and suggestions have not proven to be successful.

What is the Role of the Parent in the SST Process?

The parent:

* provides valuable information and another viewpoint for planning an effective program,

* shares the child's strengths and concerns with school staff,

* participates in the development of a positive intervention plan for their child.

My child's strengths are (interests, hobbies, skills):

Concerns for my child are:

What motivates my child is:

Expectations I have for my child are:

Student Questionnaire

My strengths are:

Things I like about school are:

My concerns are:

At Home

Ways my family helps me:

My Future

When I finish high school I want to

Jobs I would enjoy are:

Parent Preparation Questionnaire

Student Success Team

What is the Student Success Team (SST)?

Students are most successful where there is a strong spirit of cooperation between home and school.

Based on our shared responsibility, the SST meets at school to explore possibilities and strategies that will best meet the educational needs of your student.

How does it Work?

The Process:

Students are typically referred by the classroom teacher, but any member of the school staff may request support from the SST for a student whose learning, behavior or emotional needs are not being met under existing circumstances.

Prior to the first formal SST meeting, teachers have met to review classroom modifications that enhance learning for students. A modification may be as simple as a change in seating location, a daily assignment sheet, or an increase in the use of visual teaching aids. Sometimes a simple change can make a big difference for a student.

Any modification that has been tried or is currently in place will be discussed with you at the SST meeting. Using this information, the team can suggest further steps to help the student.

The Student Success Team Meeting:

Staff members will come prepared with information about your student. Information may include work samples, attendance records or assessment results. All information will be listed on the **SST Summary Form.**

The SST Summary will contain areas of:

- Student Strengths
- Information
- Modifications
- Areas of Concern
- Questions
- Strategies
- Action
- Responsible Person(s)

Other members of the team may include support staff such as: a nurse or psychologist and a meeting facilitator.

SST SUMMARY FORM

STUDENT: _____ SCHOOL: _____ TEAM: _____ DATE OF INITIAL SST: _____

PRIMARY LANGUAGE: _____ GRADE: _____ BIRTHDATE: _____ PARENTS: _____

| STRENGTHS | KNOWN | | CONCERNS Prioritize | QUESTIONS | STRATEGIES Brainstorm | ACTIONS (Prioritize) | Who | When |
	Information	Modifications						

Follow Up Date: _____ *Invite:* _____

Team Members' Signature & Position:

1. Parent _____
2. Student _____
3. Administrator _____
4. Referring Teacher _____

5. _____
6. _____
7. _____
8. _____

SST SUMMARY FORM

STUDENT: _Joe Smith_   SCHOOL: _Honeydale_   TEAM: _"B"_   DATE OF INITIAL SST: _10/15/97_

PRIMARY LANGUAGE: _English_   GRADE: _6_   BIRTHDATE: _5/6/86_   PARENTS: _Mrs. Smith_

STRENGTHS	KNOWN Information	KNOWN Modifications	CONCERNS Prioritize	QUESTIONS	STRATEGIES Brainstorm	ACTIONS (Prioritize)	Who	When
Comes to school	3 brothers 3 sisters	Changed seat	Poor academics and behavior problems	How many brothers and sisters in family?	Peer helper	Counseling	Ms. Jones	Continue
Nice smile	failing in all subjects	Modified work	No friends		Do homework	Peer helper		
					Improve behavior	Modify work		
					Get counseling			

Add specific strengths, include preferences, incentives, and potential career interests. A more helpful comment would be "positive peer relationships."

Information should be neutral, comments should not be listed in this column.

Modifications should be rated with a + or a − for their effectiveness

Be descriptive. Prioritize major concerns. There should be more strengths than concerns.

This should be a team member opportunity to note questions that came up in the process.

Strategies should be "HOW TO" ideas and positive in nature.

Choose from 2-4 NEW strategies.

List specific dates. Continue and ASAP are not adequate information.

Do not hold staff responsible for action if they are not in attendance at the meeting.

No follow-up date set.

SST meetings ALWAYS include parent. Other team members did not sign protocol.

Follow Up Date:

Invite:

Team Members' Signature & Position:

1. Parent _____ _Not present_ _____
2. Student _____ _Joe Smith_ _____
3. Administrator _____ _Mr. Dan_ _____
4. Referring Teacher _____
5. _____ / _____
6. _____ / _____
7. _____ / _____
8. _____ / _____

EXAMPLE OF A SERIOUSLY LIMITED PROCESS

Summary Form Example 2

SST SUMMARY FORM

STUDENT: _Lorena Lopez_   SCHOOL: _Clearwater_   TEAM: _"SST3"_   DATE OF INITIAL SST: _March 31, 1997_

PRIMARY LANGUAGE: _English_   GRADE: _7_   BIRTHDATE: _1/25/85_   PARENTS: _Navidad & Jorge Lopez_

STRENGTHS	KNOWN Information	Modifications	CONCERNS Prioritize	QUESTIONS	STRATEGIES Brainstorm	ACTIONS (Prioritize)	Who	When
Great dancer	Family- Lives with mom and 13-yr-old brother	+ one-to-one tutor for English + met with mom	② Not staying on task – talking	Does she have a hearing problem?	1-Counseling at church	Counseling at church	Mom and student	By 4/15
Break dancer					1-Time-out place in class			
POP	School- 3 elementary schools	- seat change - suspended 3 times - Saturday school	① Verbal conflicts with some peers and some staff	An auditory processing problem?	2-summer school	Counseling will contact home	Counselor	By 4/30
Likes science					2-homework center	Teacher will set up	Teacher	By 4/12
Good attendance		+ Uncle helping with math		Does she need glasses	2- Daily planner	Student will purchase and use	Student	By 4/12
Supportive family			③ Academics – Falling behind, especially English Comprehension weak		2-re-check vision and hearing	Mom will set up appointment	Mom	By 4/12
Likes to read	Grades- Soc. Studies-D							
Risk taker	English-F Math-D PE-C				2-quiet place to work with aunt at home	Mom and aunt will help set up	Mom	By 4/30
Enjoys helping young children	Health- Glasses in 4th grade. Ear aches as a child Normal birth Physical 3 years ago				2-librarycard	Dad		
Works hard								

Follow Up Date: _May 15, 1997_   Invite: _both mom and dad and aunt_

Team Members' Signature & Position:

1. Parent _Navidad Lopez_   5. ___ _Guilda Lowenstein_ ___ _Teacher_
2. Student _Lorena Lopez_   6. ___ _Mel Jurisch_ ___ _ORC_
3. Administrator _Michelle Allen_   7. ___ _Belinda Guterrez_ ___
4. Referring Teacher _Barney Scnorr_   8. ___ _Nurse_ ___

Example of an Exemplary SST Summary Form

Summary Form Example 3

123

SST FOLLOW UP FORM

STUDENT: _____ SCHOOL: _____ TEAM: _____ DATE OF INITIAL SST: _____

PRIMARY LANGUAGE: _____ GRADE: _____ BIRTHDATE: _____ PARENTS: _____

NEW INFORMATION	PREVIOUS ACTIONS	OUTCOMES	NEW ACTIONS	Who	When

Follow-up Date: _____ *Invite:* _____

Team Members' Signature & Position:

1. Parent _____

2. Student _____

3. Administrator _____

4. Referring Teacher _____

5. _____ / _____

6. _____ / _____

7. _____ / _____

8. _____ / _____

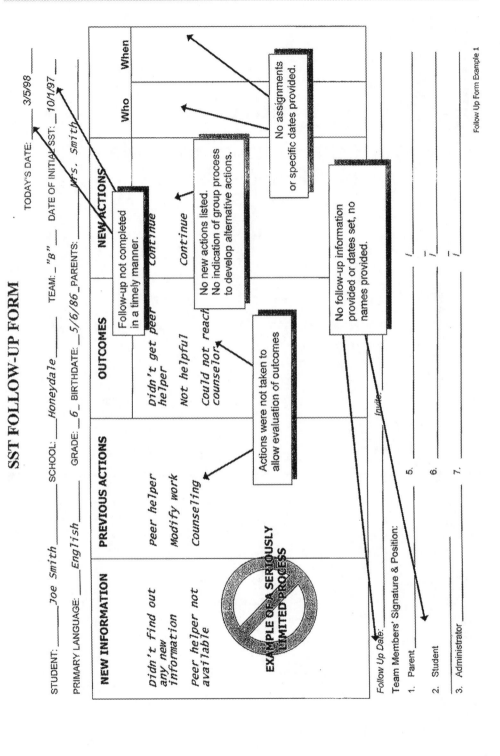

SST FOLLOW-UP FORM

STUDENT: _Joe Smith_ SCHOOL: _Honeydale_ TEAM: _"B"_ DATE OF INITIAL SST: _10/1/97_ TODAY'S DATE: _3/5/98_

PRIMARY LANGUAGE: _English_ GRADE: _6_ BIRTHDATE: _5/6/86_ PARENTS: _Mrs. Smith_

NEW INFORMATION	PREVIOUS ACTIONS	OUTCOMES	NEW ACTIONS		
				Who	When
Didn't find out any new information	Peer helper	Didn't get peer helper	Continue		
Peer helper not available	Modify work	Not helpful	Continue		
	Counseling	Could not reach counselor			

Follow-up not completed in a timely manner.

No new actions listed. No indication of group process to develop alternative actions.

No assignments or specific dates provided.

Actions were not taken to allow evaluation of outcomes

No follow-up information provided or dates set, no names provided

EXAMPLE OF A SERIOUSLY LIMITED PROCESS

Follow Up Date: _____

Team Members' Signature & Position:

1. Parent _____
2. Student _____
3. Administrator _____
5. _____
6. _____
7. _____

Invite

Follow Up Form Example 1

125

Appendix 3

School Attendance Review Team (SART) Appendix

1. Example of a SART Contract, BUSD.

The following additional SST forms and documents can be downloaded from www. routledge.com/9781032146294.

BERKELEY UNIFIED SCHOOL DISTRICT
School Attendance Review Board Mediation
Attendance Contract for Student and Family

California Education Code Section 48262 – Habitual Truant: Any pupil/student deemed a habitual truant and who has been reported as a truant three or more times per school year, provided that no pupil/student shall be deemed a habitual truant unless an appropriate district officer or employee has made a conscientious effort to hold at least one conference with the parent or guardian of the pupil/student and the student himself or herself after filing of either of the reports required under California Education Code Section 48260 or 48261.

Consistent with the above regulations from the California Education Code, your child, our student, has been declared a "habitual truant". The efforts undertaken by the school to this point have not been effective. If this pattern cannot change at this level, the next step is to refer the matter to the Alameda County District Attorney that may lead to a hearing before a judge who has a number of options at his or her discretion. Based on this conference, we have agreed to the following actions.

Student shall:

1. Attend the entire school day, each and every day, and come prepared to participate.
2. Follow all school rules and regulations and maintain good behavior in the classroom, on campus, to and from school. (EC 48200 and 48260).
3. Take individual responsibility to prepare for school each day, including assigned homework.
4. _____
5. _____
6. _____

Parent(s)/Guardian(s) shall:

1. Acknowledge that it is your legal responsibility to see that your child attend school regularly.
2. Attend all school meetings and conferences concerning your child.
3. Verify all absences with the school on the morning of the absence.
4. Present to the school a note from a medical professional to verify any past or future absence due to illness or a medical procedure.
5. _____
6. _____
7. _____
8. _____

School shall:

1. Keep the student's record of attendance current, accurate and available.
2. Send an updated attendance printout/information to the SARB facilitator for 14 day review.
3. Report any noncompliance with the SARB contractual agreement to BUSD Student Services.
4. _____
5. _____
6. _____
7. _____

Student Attendance Review Board shall:

1. Refer the parent(s)/guardian(s) to the District Attorney's office if the SARB contract is broken.
2. _____
3. _____
4. _____

Parent(s)/Guardian(s): I/We consent to the participation of my/our child under the agreement above, and I/we will cooperate and support the program as outlined. I/we further consent to the exchange of student records between the school and services/resources to which my/our child is referred.

Parent(s)/Guardian(s) Signature: _____ date: _____

Student: I have received a copy of this agreement and understand the terms and agree to comply with all the conditions above.

Student signature: _____ date: _____

SARB Administrator signature: _____ date: _____

Follow-up due on the following date: _____

Printed in the United States
by Baker & Taylor Publisher Services